THE FORK

Inspirational

Poems

for

Christians

Written and illustrated

by R. Wayne Edwards

Cover design

by Ron Edwards

THE FORK
Copyright © 2007 by FamilyPoet.Com

Cover design by Ron Edwards

ISBN 0-9743803-5-0

To Ruth, my wife, whose insistence that I write one book of serious poetry brought this book into existence.

Back cover photo
The author and two of his granddaughters:
Alyssa and Ashlyn

INTRODUCTION

When I started writing poetry, I would take a Bible character from one of the well-known Bible stories and embellish what we know about him or her to make an interesting story. It was fun to let the grandkids try to see how quickly they could guess who the poem was about. I wrote a few funny poems right from the beginning but my first efforts were more of a serious nature. I looked back through my files and discovered that I have more than enough poems to fill a book of inspirational poems. Some are Bible stories like *LUNCH*, some are political in nature like *CHOICE* and some are more the warm fuzzy type like *THE ROSE*, while some are intended to teach a moral lesson like *THE SERMON*. Then there are poems just to make you think, like *AFTER LIFE* and *HOMECOMING*.

You have heard many of the stories before. I certainly didn't make up the Bible stories but the poetry is all original and is 100% mine. Even though I put this disclaimer in all of my books I still hear comments from readers saying that I was claiming to have originated a story that they have heard before. Of course, many of my poems are completely original and I am sure that someone else will some day change some of them into their own words and perpetuate them down through time.

When I took the required literature courses in college, the instructor would spend hours giving us his opinion of just what a poet meant. Not that anyone will ever teach a class on my poetry but I have decided to make it easy if anyone ever does. I have followed each of the poems in this book with the moral lesson that I intended to convey. These little essays contain quite a bit of my family history for those readers who, like me, always wonder what kind of a person the author was, of a book that I liked.

I have included my web site in the hope that you will be interested enough in my writing to look at other work that I have done. You might even write and say nice things about what you have read. (Honest criticism will also be considered.)

Wayne Edwards

MORAL

Everything has
A moral behind it,
If only one
Can find it.

THE FORK

"A fork," the preacher said,
Condescension in his voice,
"Of all your earthly goods,
A fork's to be your choice?"

She had asked him for a visit,
For she was going to die.
They had talked about her service,
How she wanted none to cry.

She would be in her church dress
With a fork placed in her hand.
"But why a fork?" His curiosity
Was more than he could stand.

Her eyes no longer focused
But she hadn't lost her smile.
She made a place beside her
And said, "Come and sit a while."

Then she began to tell
Of the years she'd lived alone;
Old friends no longer visited,
Very few would even phone.

When you have no one to eat with,
You hardly ever cook.
You curl up on the couch
With a sandwich and a book.

You dream of childhood times,
When Mother's cooking was a treat.
She knew just how to cook
All the things we liked to eat.

Afterwards we'd clear the table
And wipe up every crumb.
But we knew to keep our forks,
'Cause the best was yet to come.

If I had to eat liver
Or spilled gravy on my skirt,
All that would be forgotten
When Mom brought out dessert.

My life was not the greatest,
As for good times I've had some,
But I'm going to keep my fork
'Cause the best is yet to come.

The Fork

This is the kind of story that I love to turn into a poem. It is a real tearjerker but still has a touch of humor. The lady had been saving her fork for a long time and she was looking forward to her dessert. The moral of the story is quite evident. When things look grim and you wonder if it is worth it all, just hang on to that fork. There is always the promise of a rainbow after a storm.

THE LUNCH

My mother could make such a wonderful lunch,
With sandwiches so tasty and chips you could munch.
Each sandwich was full of all she could cram,
With all kinds of meats but of course never ham.

Now this was to be a most special day
With no time to dawdle and no time to play.
The lunch was to last from morning 'til night,
So mother made sure she got everything right.

She gave it to me as I went out the door
And then she said, "Wait, there's one package more.
It's the scraps that were left from supper last night.
We never waste food, it just isn't right.

So if you have time and it won't make you late,
Just give it to the boy who begs at the gate. "
When I went through the gate, the boy was right there
But to give him those scraps, just didn't seem fair.

He was dirty and skinny and he must have been cold,
For the clothes that he wore were tattered and old.
So I gave him my jacket and I gave him my lunch
With my two tasty sandwiches and the chips you can munch.

I knew I'd be hungry, for the day would be long,
But it made me feel good, in my heart was a song.
He said not a word but his look was enough,
In his eye was a tear, he wasn't so tough.

So I went on my way and my steps felt so light
And if I got hungry, I had scraps from last night.
Today I would see him, he's in all the news,
This man that some call, the King of the Jews.

They said he would speak on the side of the hill,
If I can just hear him, it'll be such a thrill.
I knew they would be there, the poor and the proud,
But never before had I seen such a crowd.

Once more I began to think about food,
Just how would the Master feed this multitude?
But I'm sure you now know how the people were fed.
In my bag were two fishes and five scraps of bread.

The Lunch

Now this one was fun. It was easy to write and I got my O'Henry ending in with no problem. I put the exact scripture that I used at the bottom of the poem because there are slightly different versions in the different gospels.

None of the writers, however, tell us anything of the boy that shared his lunch with Jesus that day. Wouldn't it be fun to know something about him? I claim no divine revelation but I think he would be pleased with my version of what must have been the most memorable day in his life.

John 6:9

AFTERLIFE

Two young brothers lay side by side,
Pondering the meaning of life.
There was Believer so full of joy
And Doubter who focused on strife.

Believer could hear the voice of God,
It filled his thoughts with wonder.
Doubter would say, "That wasn't God,
All that you heard was thunder."

Doubter was happy, or so he thought,
He was sure there was nothing more.
But Believer just knew there was more after life
And allowed all his thoughts to soar.

"You're foolish to believe there's anything more,"
Pessimistic Doubter would say.
But the faith of Believer, so pure and so strong,
Not even Doubter could sway.

Doubter would say, that when his time comes,
He'll resist with kicking and screaming.
But it's such a bright and splendid abode,
The one of which Believer's been dreaming.

Remember, though life is important,
That we're only here for a season.
And when we each meet our Maker,
Then we'll understand the reason.

Their time had grown short, was the one thing
Both brothers had come to agree.
A future both bleak and foreboding
Was all that poor Doubter could see.

While Believer, with anticipation,
Would leave his domain without sorrow;
Doubter, who thought it the end,
Had no splendid dreams of tomorrow.

When the time for Believer had come,
He went through a tunnel towards light
And there in wonder and awe
Met a being all dressed up in white.

But Doubter, with much trepidation,
Had watched his brother pass on
And he knew that his life, too, was over,
Any hopes of a future were gone.

While out in a world, filled with marvelous light,
Beautiful beings were gathered around.
Believer was seeing most wonderful sights
And hearing such wonderful sound.

And then he was laid to his mother's warm breast
With such tender love and care.
The doctor was saying, "There's no time to rest,
There's another one she has to bear".

One more to be born but he's fighting so,
He's pulled right out of my reach.
The doctor then said, to the ones in the room,
"It looks like he's gonna be breech!"

So if you believe, like Doubter,
That when you are dead you are dead,
You might give a thought to Believer
And ponder what's lying ahead.

Afterlife

We, in all of our wisdom and knowledge, have little idea what our afterlife will bring us any more than does the fetus living so comfortably in his mother's womb. Oh, from time to time, he hears things and may see the light of the outside world through the skin of his mother's tummy. It sort of reminds you of what the Bible teaches in I Corinthians 13:12, which reads, "For now we see through a glass darkly; but then face to face: now I know in part; but then shall I know even as I am known." We, like the one twin, can prepare for an afterlife of beauty and wonder or like his brother, we can face our eternity kicking and screaming.

A VERY SPECIAL ANGEL

There would be a celebration;
A child would soon be born.
All of the angels would be there,
Even Gabriel with his horn.

But the child asked the Creator,
"Why must I be sent to Earth?
I am so completely helpless,
Why must I experience birth?"

God said, "There will be an angel
To be with you all the way.
An angel to protect and love you
From your very first Earth day."

The child said, "I will miss it here,
This place so full of light and song."
God said, "Your angel's song will soothe you,
So your nights will not seem long."

He said, "Your angel then will teach you
All of the things you need to know
To make your life a fruitful one
While you spend it down below."

"But God, I know I'll surely miss You,
I know how much I'll have to say."
"When you need to talk to me
Your angel will teach you how to pray."

"My angel sounds so very special,
That you created just for me.
But just how can an angel love
Someone as helpless as I'll be?"

"Your angel's life will be for you
And you will fill your angel's heart
On the very day you're born,
'Cause then your angel's life will start."

"But just what is my angel's name?
How will I know it from another?"
"Your angel has an earthly name
But you will learn to call her Mother."

A Very Special Angel

There is no Biblical backing for a pre-existence. God did say that he knew us in our mother's womb. Some religions believe that we all had a life before being conceived on Earth and that our earthly status is earned during this pre-existence. I haven't changed religions but I did think the concept was interesting enough to write a poem about. *A Very Special Angel* was written as a Mother's Day poem and not as a statement of belief. In my humorous poems, I quite often write stories about Heaven and Hell that certainly don't reflect my beliefs. If you belong to a religion that teaches pre-existence, I hope that this poem will have special meaning for you.

THE ALARM

Would you believe that dumb alarm,
It failed to work again.
Sam would be late another time,
Just like he'd usually been.

He'd bought it from a peddler,
It had no guarantee.
It would have cost too much
Had the peddler made it free!

The peddler said that this alarm
Was sure to be a winner.
If it didn't work tomorrow,
He'd have the thing for dinner.

Sam stayed up way too late,
Around the court yard fire.
When there's so much excitement,
One seldom seems to tire.

The man had answered far too quickly
And you could see his fear.
When Sam had said, "I saw you
Cut off that fellow's ear."

"It wasn't me, I wasn't there",
But Sam could tell he lied.
The angry curses, hard to fake,
No matter how he tried.

Sam had a hard time leaving;
The courtyard fire was warm.
He didn't know how he'd wake up
Without a good alarm.

Sam didn't hear the stupid rooster,
But one thing that we know,
Down in the courtyard by the fire,
A man named Peter heard him crow.

The Alarm

You won't appreciate a rooster for an alarm clock unless you've lived in the country. There are advantages and disadvantages: they work during power failures and you don't have to remember to set them, but they know nothing about daylight saving time and they can't be un-set for weekends and holidays. You also have to worry about night predators, such as the fox, coon or owl, turning your alarm off prematurely. I thought it would be interesting to make up a story about one of the possible courtyard bystanders on the night Peter denied knowing Jesus, not from any perspective of how it might have changed his life from his close encounter with Jesus and Peter, but that life goes on, even with the unbeliever.

Matthew 26:34

THE AQUARIUM

Why had God taken my best friend?
An awful thing he'd done to me.
I needed John more than He did,
A loving God would surely see.

A world that is full of sinners,
He could have taken one of those.
Or the beggar on the corner
With the pathetic smelly clothes?

My best friend John was full of love,
A life of service carefully planned.
His passage bought, all set to go,
To serve God in a foreign land.

No loving God could be so cruel,
A thing that I could not forgive.
Why did he take a Christian's life
And let so many sinners live?

As I sat there in abject sorrow,
Wrapped up in pity for myself,
I noticed the aquarium
That I had placed on my bookshelf.

I saw the guppy that I'd picked
To be used in my perfect plan.
His large tail, so brightly colored,
In the shape of a fancy fan.

I got my net and caught him out.
He was the one that I would need.
The one to improve the color
Of all the guppies that I breed.

Right then a thought occurred to me,
I had no clue what God had planned.
When I caught out my perfect fish,
The guppies didn't understand.

Aquarium

This is a poem that I wrote after our young pastor passed away. His death was especially hard on the youth of the church. He had been the youth pastor before becoming the senior pastor and all of the young people loved him. A woman in our Sunday school class asked how to explain God's taking of our pastor, to her daughter. Her daughter had asked why God took a person with so much potential and left another person in the church who was retarded. I knew that her daughter kept tropical fish and I told her to use them as an illustration. I came home and wrote this poem. Maybe it will be of help to you some day, when it comes your time to explain why God allowed the loss of a friend.

ASK AND YOU SHALL RECEIVE

He asked God for a mansion
with a butler and a maid.
He got a mobile home
with a mortgage to be paid.
He asked God for a cathedral
with a steeple and a bell.
He got a dirt floor mission
just outside the gates of Hell.
He asked God for the wisdom
to get him through each day.
He wondered what he'd get this time
but God just said, "Okay."

Ask And You Shall Receive

All of our prayers are answered. It's just that the answer is sometimes, "NO." One woman in our Sunday school class once said that if God had answered all of her prayers, she would have married the wrong man, several times. I think I'll write a poem about that. The man doing the praying, in this instance, is a preacher. A good preacher would probably be better in tune with God's plan for his life. I once saw a plaque on a preacher friend's wall; "I don't want a cathedral with a steeple and a bell. Give me a chapel just outside the gates of Hell." (But he seemed to be enjoying his plush, air-conditioned office.)

BABY JESUS

Somebody stole Baby Jesus
From the manger scene on the lawn.
The preacher, when he came to church,
Was first to find the baby gone.

He said, with anger in his voice,
That the baby had been taken
And that his faith in human kind
Was beginning to be shaken.

Right after church, still breathing flames,
Like a legendary dragon,
He met Tommy on the sidewalk
Playing with a new red wagon.

Tommy was so very happy,
It thawed the preacher's angry heart.
But what he saw in the wagon
Gave the young preacher quite a start.

"It was you stole Baby Jesus,
That was an evil thing to do!"
Tommy said, "But Brother Pastor,
I thought that everybody knew.

I asked Jesus for this wagon,"
As he patted it with pride,
"And I told him if I got it
That I would let him have first ride!"

Baby Jesus

Baby Jesus is about jumping to conclusions. Before deciding that someone has done something wrong, listen to his or her side of the story. No matter how impossible it may seem, they may have a plausible explanation. Tommy was very sure that Jesus would approve of what he was doing. After all, Tommy had made a promise.

THE BANQUET

I didn't want to tell her,
Because she thinks that I'm too soft.
I knew that when she found out,
I'd be sleeping in the loft.

The rooms have both been empty
And our business has been slow.
We really need to rent them,
Because we really need the dough.

Our nicest room was upstairs
We had fixed it up to rent.
Peter said it was the one
He was sure the Master meant.

My wife had spent long hours
Getting everything just right.
She'd set up the long table,
It was such a pretty sight.

My son had gone for water,
When he met the two, you see,
They said the Master sent them
And they had to talk to me.

One man said his name was John
And the big one's name was Pete.
They had come to get a room
Where thirteen of them could eat.

I rubbed my hands together,
I would ask a handsome price.
They'd not find another room
That was even half as nice.

So I thought it was a joke,
The kind that's never funny,
When John said they were teachers
And had no need for money.

They said they were to tell me
"The Master has need of it."
They seemed sure that I'd agree
But my wife would have a fit.

And she would surely tell me,
"Just how stupid can you be?
Tomorrow is Passover
When we double-up our fee."

I don't know what possessed me,
It would surely cause me strife.
I said that they could have it
But how would I tell my wife?

Well now I had to face her
And tell her what I had done.
I took a bunch of flowers,
It sure would not be fun.

I made sure when I told her,
That she didn't have her broom.
She said, "Don't you think I knew?
Jesus needs THE UPPER ROOM!"

Banquet

When I read one of my Bible Story poems to children, I like to see how soon they can guess the Bible story that it is about. When I read the title of this poem, my grandson, Ryan, said, "It's about the Last Supper isn't it?" Have you ever wondered what people thought when they came in contact with Jesus? What would you have said if two strangers had come up to you and told you that the Master needed your room for the night? Jesus could have provided money for the room. He could have gotten it out of a fish's mouth, like he did on another occasion, but it would have robbed the owner of a blessing. Unlike the claims of some TV evangelists, we should not always expect to glean huge returns on the gifts we give to God.

Luke 22:7-13

BURDEN

His neighbor was important
For he knew all the elite.
He was always quick to brag
About someone he would meet.

He told Simon of the stars
That he hobnobbed with each day;
That when he went to eat out,
How they wouldn't let him pay.

Simon was a common man
Who worked hard for a living
And everyone who knew him
Said he was kind and giving.

His neighbor, the exception,
He thought Simon was just dumb.
Why else would he give money
To every passing bum?

Why would he spend so much time
Carrying food to the sick?
It is not the kind of fun
That a normal man would pick.

So the neighbor couldn't wait
To taunt Simon every day.
He would ask whom he had "helped"
And how much he gave away.

Since this was Friday morning,
Simon had too much to do.
He gathered up some firewood
For a widow that he knew.

But, as he drove into town,
His way was blocked by a throng.
People watched a prisoner
Dragging quite a load along.

His wounds showed he'd been beaten
And He stumbled with his load.
Simon pulled his cart over,
So he wouldn't block the road.

He saw the prisoner's guards
Were in an ugly mood.
He mustn't make them angry,
He knew they'd be more than rude.

And then Simon saw the eyes,
Eyes that he would not forget.
He had to get much closer,
Just as close as they would let.

The face, though beaten and bruised,
Was still full of love and care.
A crown of thorns was tangled,
In His bloody matted hair.

Simon saw the heavy load
Was more than the man could bear.
It wasn't just the timber,
He was loaded down with care.

Then the prisoner stumbled
And fell down upon his knee.
No way that he could make it,
Couldn't anybody see?

The soldier yelled, "Get going!"
And prodded him with his spear.
Then Simon lost his senses
And completely lost his fear.

Simon had to help this man,
For he knew he'd done no wrong.
The soldier stopped his goading
When he burst in through the throng.

Then all the guards came running
To fend off Simon's attack.
But Simon just took the load
From off the prisoner's back.

When Simon watched them nail Him
To the cross made from a tree,
He knew that he was giving
Up his life for you and me.

Then that night, while Simon worked
Out beneath the sun's last ray,
His neighbor came to chastise
And ask him about his day.

Simon said, "You would just think
That my whole day was a loss,
Since the only thing I did
Was to carry someone's cross."

Burden

We actually know quite a bit about Simon. We know his name, where he came from and what he was doing. The writers of the gospels indicate that he was forced into duty but do you think that they would have given as much information as they did about an unwilling person? At any rate, here is a complete rundown of just how his day went. If you don't believe that it happened this way, then feel free to write your own version.

Mark 15:21

THE CASUALTY OF CHRISTMAS

The store clerk saw the Stranger,
And the sad look on His face,
As he watched Christmas shoppers
Rush around from place to place.

The next time that he saw Him,
He was by the manger scene,
Some people had thrown trash there
And it wasn't kept too clean.

Then he watched Him make His way
Through the present wrapping line,
So that he could get a look
At the Merry Xmas sign.

He just stood there by the X
With a teardrop on His cheek.
The store clerk had to wonder
What this man had come to seek.

There was a look of sadness
On His face, when He would pause
To watch the line of children
Tell how they loved Santa Claus.

And then a Blue Light Special,
A new toy was put on sale,
Stampeding wild-eyed shoppers
Caught the Stranger in their swell.

That night they found His body
Mangled by the hectic crush
Of many Christmas shoppers'
Frantic, bargain-hunting rush.

What had caused the Stranger's death
On this happy Christmas Eve?
Would there be someone to care
Or would anybody grieve?

The coroner said the man
Had been trampled 'til He died.
But had no explanation
For the knife wound in His side.

Two marks that mystified him,
And caused the coroner's qualm,
Were the jagged puncture wounds
In the center of each palm.

MERRY XMAS

TALK
TO
SANTA

The Casuality Of Christmas

The Casualty of Christmas is, of course, a parody. Our children learn about Santa Claus before they learn about whose birthday Christmas is. I know that we are constantly told that X is a symbol for God but isn't that just an attempt to appease those of us who are Christians? Xmas just doesn't quite do it for me. I'm not preaching against Santa Claus, I just think that he shouldn't be allowed to overshadow the birthday Child.

THE CHOICE

Just a slip of a girl
From a very small town,
Where the gossip was quick
To drag anyone down.

A girl that was single
Was having a baby.
It was surely a sin,
No if, and, or maybe.

No way to explain
An illegitimate child
And the rumors were swift,
They'd begun to run wild.

She had led a good life
And had tried not to sin
But her neighbors now thought
How terrible she'd been.

The man she would marry,
What's he going to say?
Just how could she tell him?
It would sure ruin his day.

No DNA testing
But no need to bother
'Cause she knew her betrothed
Could not be the father.

She was such a young girl,
At this time in her life,
That a baby would cause
Her a whole lot of strife.

A quick marriage was planned
And a trip far away.
He was a carpenter
Who made very poor pay.

So if he would have her,
Considering her plight,
They might still not survive
With a budget so tight.

He was a good person,
Such a very nice man,
But everyone wondered
Whether he'd understand.

All her friends were too quick
With unwanted advice.
No good man would want her,
Even one that was nice.

Before someone tells him,
There is no need for doubt,
As friends we must tell you
Take the easy way out.

You know its just tissue,
It's not yet become life,
So why should it cause you
So much unneeded strife?

But she knew what they called,
Only fetal demise,
Was the death of a child
In her God's holy eyes.

And for this special child
What a sin it would be
And not just against God,
But all humanity.

What a terrible world
Of hate and distortion,
If Mary of Nazareth
Had had an abortion.

Choice

Well, it's time to get serious. This poem clearly shows what my feelings are on abortion. I read a list somewhere, of all of the famous people who would have probably been aborted had their mothers had access to the procedure. Who knows how many of God's wounderful plans for humanity have been aborted along with the millions of fetuses? When I wrote this poem, it was my hope that it could be of use, in some small way, by anyone involved in pro-life. If it can be used in any way to save the lives of unborn babies, I freely give my permission.

CHRISTMAS GIFT

I would find the perfect gift,
I knew nothing else would do.
It had to be so special
To show that my love was true.

So I went from store to store
And I saw so many things.
I set myself no limits,
Even looked at diamond rings.

Now the perfect gift for her
Must tell just how much I feel,
And must leave no shred of doubt
That my love for her is real.

The days that I spent looking
For the perfect gift were long.
The thoughts of her excitement
Put into my heart a song.

Then I found the perfect gift
In a dingy little store.
It was just the kind of place
Fancy people would ignore.

I didn't wrap it fancy,
For the gift alone was such
That it would convey my love,
She would understand how much.

It was all that I could do
Just to wait for Christmas Day.
In my mind, a hundred times,
I had guessed what she would say.

It was a little early
When I drove out to her place.
My gift with its plain wrapping,
No ribbon or fancy lace.

With shaking hands, I gave her
The gift I had bought with care.
She looked at the box and asked,
"Did it really come from there?"

"So many fancy places
Why not shop at one of those?
Nothing good comes from that place,
As any fool surely knows!"

Of course my heart was broken.
I had never felt so low.
I got back into my car
And I drove away real slow.

With a heart so full of grief,
Grief that set my thoughts adrift.
Did we too respond in kind
To our God's most perfect gift?

Christmas Gift

My wife Ruth, looks forward to Christmas because she loves to give gifts. She always seems to know what would be perfect for whom. It's not as much fun for her though, if she can't be there to see it being opened. It takes all of the fun out of her giving if there is a negative or a ho-hum reaction. I'm sure that you saw right away that *Christmas Gift* is a parody. It's about what God's reaction must be when we reject His gift.

WORRY

I met Death coming toward our town
So I stopped him and asked him why...
He told me that one hundred souls,
In our town, had been picked to die.

I rushed back to tell the people.
I had to warn all of my friends,
To let them know one hundred souls
Were picked by Death to meet their ends.

One hundred people, Death had said,
Instead, one thousand souls had died.
I ran and caught Death as he left
To make him tell me why he'd lied.

He said he had no time for me,
Death is always in a hurry.
He claimed he took a hundred souls,
All the others died of worry.

Worry

It is a scientific fact that worry can cause early death. The nine hundred people in this poem that weren't scheduled to die worried so much that they joined the hundred that were scheduled. In the true Christian's vocabulary, the word worry should be replaced with concern. A Christian should have no worry in his life because he knows that God is in charge. Of course, the other extreme is the attitude of the Christian who thinks that since God is in charge, no action is required on his or her part. I've heard the Christian parent say, "I'm really too busy to spend a lot of time with my children, I've committed them to God and he will take care of them." Concern is a Christian's responsibility.

CREATOR

Two little wooden dolls lay drying,
Side by side on a wooden table.
One doll decided his name was Cain,
The other doll had chosen Abel.

Cain asked Abel, "How did we get here?
I wonder how we came to evolve?"
Abel said, that someone had made them,
"That's no difficult problem to solve."

But Cain had different ideas
Of how the two of them came about.
"No one could ever have made my form,
Of that I have not one little doubt."

Abel said, "But just look at us two,
A head, two arms, two eyes and two legs.
Someone has made us in his image,
We didn't just evolve out of dregs."

But Cain was right, he was so certain,
He told Abel how they'd come to be.
Random lightning had struck a tree limb
"When I explain, I'm sure you will see."

"But look, we're so wonderfully made,
There was surely a masterful plan."
But Cain said, "No way, I am certain
That no being made THIS wooden man."

I fell out of a tree as a twig
And then tumbled about on the ground.
Sand, pebbles and rocks, placed at random,
Carved and polished me 'til I was round.

Then the rainwater caused me to swell
So that my legs and arms split apart.
Then the sun caused my pigmentation.
I'm the result of Ma Natures art."

Abel said, "Now that's convoluted.
For your ideas, I wouldn't trade.
It's much simpler to believe like me,
That we are most wonderfully made."

They argued all day in the sunlight,
As they lay talking there, side by side.
Each so sure of his own origin,
No compromise would either abide.

Just then a shadow loomed over them
And something gave each doll a light touch,
"I wonder why the paint isn't dry.
I wonder if I put on too much."

He turned them once more in the sunlight,
In the hopes that they soon would be dry.
When he had gone, Cain said to Abel,
"Well I wonder, just who was that guy?"

Creator

The evolutionists tell us that from whales to cockroaches, we all came form the same primordial muck. The creationists struggle with the age-old paradox, "Who created God?" The question is just as unanswerable as, "Who created the matter that life supposedly sprang from?" Scientists are now championing the Big Bang Theory. We celebrate Independence Day with lots of fireworks. Every time there was a big bang, someone was there to light the fuse. I like to think of the way my Grandfather put it. "If they are right, what have I lost? I have led a happy fulfilling life and have been a much better person as a result of my moral convictions. If I am right they have forfeited eternity." As the Bible says, put that in the balance and weigh it.

DO YOU HAVE FROGS?

Last night, in bed, I heard from God,
He talked to me about my fate.
He said he had a plan for me.
I quickly asked if it could wait.

I said that things were not too bad,
That I could make it all alone.
The problems facing me in life,
I'd like to handle on my own.

I didn't want to pay the price,
The things I knew I had to do,
To live within the will of God
To make his promises come true.

I put him off another time,
Knowing it would cause me sorrow.
I told him that I needed help,
Just not now, perhaps tomorrow.

When I opened up my Bible,
Several scriptures caught my sight.
They were about Egyptian plagues
And the Israeli people's plight.

I read at length about each plague
And how God hardened Pharaoh's heart.
One thing I couldn't understand,
Old Pharaoh wasn't very smart.

Moses asked the stupid Pharaoh
When he would like the frogs to go.
The answer that the Pharaoh gave
Proved him to be a little slow.

When nose deep in a plague of frogs,
Just why would anybody say,
"Not right now, perhaps tomorrow,
We'd like to suffer one more day"?

Do You Have Frogs?

When Pharaoh asked Moses to pray that God would remove the plague of frogs, Moses asked when Pharaoh would like for God to make them gone. Pharaoh's answer always mystified me. Why wait until tomorrow? I would have said, "Yesterday!" But aren't we all like the person in this poem? Too often we tell God, "Not just yet God, I'm not quite ready." God entreats us to lay all of our burdens on him and he will give us rest. Check and see, are you keeping any unnecessary frogs?

Exodus 8:10

DON'T MAKE AN EAGLE MAD

Don't make an eagle mad,
The last thing one should do.
She has an awesome beak
And awesome talons too.

She is a peaceful bird
Until her nest is breached.
Then she is quick to strike
'Fore safety can be reached.

The enemy dispatched,
The nest which once stood high
Will quickly be rebuilt;
A beacon in the sky.

The eagle will remain
A symbol of the best.
Her vigilance intensified
For safety of her nest.

And those who once had dared
Are sorry that they had.
The lesson that they learned?
Don't make an eagle mad.

Don't Make An Eagle Mad

The day after the attack on our nation, on 9/11, I got a call from the secretary of my writer's guild asking me if I would write a poem about the tragedy for our newsletter. It only took me about ten minutes to do so. It just all seemed to fall in place. I wrote several other poems about patriotism but this will be the only one that I will include in *The Fork.*

EMPTY CHAIR

Daddy had an empty chair
Sitting right next to his bed.
No one knew why it was there
Because Daddy never said.

The old chair had first appeared
After Mother passed away.
It was part of Daddy's life
Ever since that awful day.

Then Dad had a heart attack,
None of us kids had been there.
The strange thing, when they found him,
His head was in that old chair.

At the funeral service,
An old friend stood up to say
That he had been with Daddy
The night Dad had learned to pray.

He said that Dad had told him,
The day that our mother died,
That when he would try to pray,
He would always get tongue-tied.

He said that he had told Dad
He should face an empty chair.
Then when he would say his prayers,
Think of Jesus sitting there.

Then he could talk to Jesus
Like he would to a close friend.
Doing that each time he prayed,
Fear of praying would soon end.

So now we know why Daddy
Had, that night, crawled out of bed.
And we know that when he died,
In whose lap he'd placed his head.

Empty Chair

This is a story poem with a moral. It is sad that Dad didn't pass his wisdom on to his children; they might have profited by it. It is evident that the children hadn't spent enough time with their dad to learn his personal testimony; they had to find out about the chair from a friend at Dad's funeral. I missed my Dad's funeral, I had just left his side in route to Vietnam when he went home to Heaven. This is a good poem to put in your church bulletin on Father's Day.

THE EMPTY EGG

He was the slowest in his class,
The little bashful boy named Craig.
She knew he wouldn't understand
When she had handed him the egg.

But not to give him his own egg,
She felt would just be too unfair.
And if he didn't comprehend,
She knew the others wouldn't care.

Each was to fill his plastic egg
To bring for Easter Show and Tell;
Something to depict the season
That they could fit inside the shell.

Excitement showed on each child's face
As each one came with egg in hand.
Each egg held a hidden treasure
Carefully placed on Teacher's stand.

The last to place his treasure there
Was little, bashful, backward, Craig.
He slowly brought it to the front,
Reluctant to give up his egg.

As she opened up each treasure,
The child would tell the class with pride,
Just how Easter was depicted
By the object that was inside.

One egg held a packet of seeds
'Cause seeds contain the hope of life.
Another held a cactus thorn,
A symbol of His pain and strife.

She waited 'til the very last
To open up the one marked Craig.
Then quickly placed it to the side
For he had brought an empty egg.

Craig came up to join the others,
All standing there in happy line.
Without his usual stutter,
He said, "You didn't open mine?"

The teacher, lost for what to say,
In answer to Craig's woeful stare,
"But Craig, I looked inside your egg.
There's absolutely nothing there!"

His answer caused her eyes to tear,
When Craig explained it to the room,
"When Mary went down to the grave,
That's what she found in Jesus' tomb."

Empty Egg

I don't know where I first heard this story but it's been around for quite a while. It was just the kind of story that I like to make into a poem. The Bible says that out of the mouth of babes and sucklings comes praise, Matt. 21:16. I, of course, gave the little boy a name that would make my job easier since it rhymes with egg. (A poet's prerogative.) This is a wonderful poem for church secretaries to include in the church bulletin on Easter Sunday.

ALLURE

What a pretty thing, she had thought,
As she had watched it going by.
She had barely caught its movement
Out of the corner of her eye.

Then once again it passed her by.
Now a noisy irritation.
Just to reach out there and grab it
Had become a strong temptation.

Still, not enough for her to leave
Her pleasant place down in the shade.
A recent meal, and quite content
As she watched the glitter fade.

It stirred some hidden memory,
Illusive cobwebs of her mind.
The memory, one of pleasure;
Or could it be the other kind?

Then it passed by her once again.
Just what was its strange attraction?
Hypnotic glitter from the sun
Enhanced fascinating action.

She'd always led a careful life,
Especially with her diet.
A hazy lesson from her past,
If it's something new don't try it.

All others sought to let her be,
In deference to her size and age.
Now this thing caused her heart to pound
And filled her mind with mounting rage.

The stupid thing had come again,
Right there before her very face.
She would no longer tolerate
This rude invasion of her space.

She'd teach the thing a lesson now
And add it to her evening lunch.
She'd grab it in her massive jaws
And feel the satisfying crunch.

So then with lightning fury speed,
She grabbed the careless noisy snack.
Blinding pain cleared ancient cobwebs
From her memory; all came back.

In foolish youth she'd grabbed this thing
That she had ever since then spurned.
But now in heated rage forgot
The painful lesson she had learned.

She got one last but fleeting glance
Of the beauty now left behind
And then her lovely world was gone
And sudden brightness left her blind.

Two fishermen admired, in awe,
The beauty of their monster catch.
The excitement of the moment
No hole-in-one could ever match.

"I turned one loose here once before,
Because back then it was too small.
But I'll not turn this beauty back,
She's going on my bedroom wall!"

Allure

"All that glitters is not gold," was one of my mother's favorite sayings. As we get older we sometimes forget the lessons that we learned in our youth. Almost daily, in the news, we hear about another senior citizen being taken by still another scam. Here we have the sad story of a senior citizen falling for a frequently used scam. She had survived the same scam in her youth but had forgotten the pain and suffering that it had caused her. Of course, the moral of the story could be that often our sad mistake can turn out to be someone else's gain; or, another, "Fool me once, shame on you, fool me twice, shame on me."

ON THE OTHER HAND

I have a good partner
That's close as a brother.
At somebody's first glance
We look like one another.

He has all the talent,
Smartest one of us two,
He mostly leads the way
In the things that we do.

Though I'll take the lead
When we have a fist fight,
He is the only one
With the talent to write.

Even though he can't read
What he's written or signed,
Unless he is reading
For someone who is blind.

To look in the mirror,
Our differences grow dim,
'Cause he seems to be me
While I seem to be him.

When we have our coffee,
We work well as a team
Because I hold the cup
While he stirs in the cream.

We are a loving team,
To show how much we care,
We both fold together
When someone says a prayer.

When we do the laundry
I help with the folding
And when we build something
I do all the holding.

Which is one job I hate,
I don't like it a bit,
When he misses the nail
I'm the one that gets hit!

I am sure that you've guessed
And by now you must see,
Though only your left hand,
Just how much you need me!

On The Other Hand

When I had surgery on my left shoulder, I lost the use of my left hand for a month. My right hand really missed its helper. It was not real good at tying shoes by itself, even though it had led the way in the past, and was at a complete loss when applause was required. Since I had acquired the two as a pair I experienced a sharp decrease in productivity. That's when I decided to write, *On the Other Hand.*

ABANDONED

A dog sits waiting in the hot summer sun;
Too faithful to leave, too frightened to run.
He's been there for days with nothing to do
But sit by the road waiting for you.

He can't understand why you left him that day,
He thought you and he were stopping to play.
He's sure you'll come back and that's why he stays.
How long will he suffer, how many more days?

His legs have grown weak, his throat's parched and dry.
He's sick now from hunger and falls with a sigh.
He lays down his head and closes his eyes.
If you could just see how a waiting dog dies.

Abandoned

This is of necessity, a sad poem. Living in the country as we do, we never have to buy pets; people dump more than we need. In the country there may be only one or two families per square mile whereas in the city, there are several hundred. Where would logic tell you an abandoned pet would have the best chance of getting a handout and maybe be taken in? I don't advocate abandoning a pet anywhere, but surely not in the country. We have gotten cats, dogs and even a duck at one time (it was sure tastey). In abandoning their pets, the owners cowardly delegate their responsibility to another unwilling person. My neighbor says that punishment for pet abandonment should result in the owner being taken to a foreign country where he doesn't know the customs or understand the language and put out along some country road without any kind of identification. There are places that accept unwanted pets. It might cost you a few dollars, but it is the Christian thing to do.

GOD'S HOUSE

God looked down and saw his sadness
And He said, "Son, don't despair.
Just because you weren't made welcome,
When you tried to worship there."

"They are a very pious bunch,
And careful of whom they let in.
They've no love or room for sinners,
They're always quick to judge one's sin."

"Oh, they don't stop you at the door
To say that you aren't welcome there.
But no one comes to shake your hand,
Or try to let you know they care."

"One other thing I must tell you,
Before you shed more needless tears.
I'm not welcome there myself.
I've not been asked inside for years."

God's House

Let's hope that little poem isn't about your church. Ruth and I have visited churches where no one seemed to know that we were first time visitors or, at least, no one cared. Larger churches have people assigned as greeters; some are even given training. Maybe it would be good if we all took a course in being nice to people. God has been shut out of our public schools, our public buildings and our parks. He's still allowed in our churches and synagogues, but whether He feels welcome or not is up to us. Maybe you should put this little poem in your church bulletin about once a year.

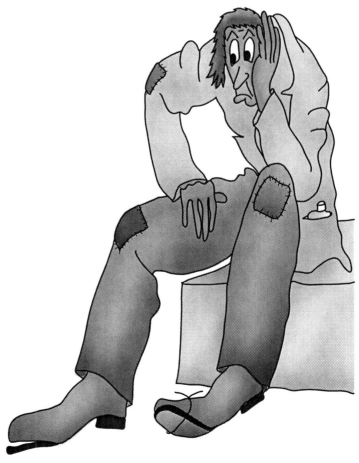

HE TOOK MY PLACE

"You can't park there," a member said,
"That parking place you took is mine."
The visitor just smiled and moved
His battered car on down the line.

He stood there in his tattered robe
With sandals on his scarred bare feet.
No one came by to shake his hand
Or show him to an empty seat.

He sat down in the nearest pew.
A member, with unfriendly face,
Then came and told the visitor,
"I guess you know you took my place."

Then later, in the vestibule,
Some noticed scars around his head
And scars on both his hands and feet
That were all deep and colored red.

When asked where all his scars came from,
On both his feet and hands and face,
He said, "I got them long ago,
The first time that I took your place."

He Took My Place

When a child says, "He took my place!", it usually has a negative connotation and is in the form of a tattle. If you ask a Christian what, "He took your place" means, it should bring up thoughts of Jesus; but at church it might have an entirely different meaning. During the not so Civil War, the wealthy could hire someone to take their place in the draft. (I always wondered who took the place of the one that was hired.) Jesus took our place for free, that's what Christianity is all about. You might remember that next Sunday, when you walk into church and find a visitor sitting where you always sit.

HERO

He was the first to smell the smoke,
It was the middle of the night,
And he was instantly awake
For surely something wasn't right.

He jumped and ran from room to room,
In each one, shouting the alarm.
His only thought, his family,
That none of them should suffer harm.

He stayed inside the burning house
'Til everyone was safe outside.
And that's why only he would hear
When little baby Billy cried.

When the family had all gathered
Just to check on one another,
Only then had they discovered
They were missing baby brother.

He rushed into the baby's room
And grabbed Billy's pajama foot.
He drug him low across the floor
Through choking smoke and fire and soot.

The heat had caught his hair afire
And set his struggling lungs aflame
But he could hear the frantic call
Of little baby Billy's name.

His dying thoughts were happy ones,
His loving family had been spared.
That he was faithful 'til the end
Was all in life for which he cared.

"No life was lost," the fire chief wrote,
While filling out his daily log,
"Unless you count the family pet,
The children's big old mongrel dog."

Hero

I bought Ruth a tiny miniature poodle to replace one that we think a bobcat or an eagle ran off with. As is the case with many small puppies, Trinket refused to eat and we had to force-feed her. That unpleasant task was, of course, Ruth's. The first few nights, Trinket spent all of her hard earned energy, telling the world how we mistreated her by taking her away from her mother. To keep her quiet, I moved her box next to the bed and slept with my hand dangling in it. As a result, she bonded with me and, whereas the first poodle was strictly Ruth's, Trinket wants to spend every waking hour with me. No human could ever give me a more enthusiastic welcome, even after I've only been gone a short time, than Trinket. Since I am six and a half feet tall and weigh two hundred and sixty pounds, Trinket would not even attempt to drag me from a burning house. She would probably just go outside and wait to enthusiastically greet me when I came out. I wrote *Hero* because a schoolteacher, who had seen my web site, wrote to me and asked if I would write a poem about heroes for her class. I thought her students would enjoy it better if it were about a dog. I didn't mean for it to turn out so sad. A lot of my poems are done by request.

HIS EYE IS ON THE SPARROW

I prayed to God without relief,
My prayers had not been getting through.
That I was praying fervently,
I wondered if God even knew.

Then driving on a lonely road,
Close in behind another car,
I saw that it had hit a bird
Left there, fluttering in the tar.

I pulled off on the gravel side,
Although it was steep and narrow.
Then I saw that the dying bird
Was a common little sparrow.

God's promise flashed before my eyes,
And so I crouched above the bird.
I knew that God would hear me now,
As it was promised in His Word.

That, even the tiny sparrow,
When it at last falls from the air,
God said He is aware of it
And He had promised to be there.

Once more my faith had been renewed,
I felt my fervent prayers take wing.
Once more I knew the kind of joy
That always makes the angels sing.

His Eye Is On The Sparrow

Matthew 10:29 tells us that when even the lowly sparrow falls, God is there. Have you ever felt that your prayers just weren't getting through? Some little assistance, even from a dead sparrow, might be all that you need to build your faith and send your prayers on their way. The man in the poem knew his Bible. He knew his God and he evidently had faith or he wouldn't have kept trying. God recognizes the need for help in our worship and prayers or He wouldn't have stressed the point that He would be there when two or three are gathered in His name. Of course He is there for you always, but Christian friends sure seem to make it easier.

Matthew 10-29

HOMECOMING

Oh, our hearts are filled with joy
For our master's coming soon.
It may be in the morning,
Tonight, or today at noon.

He left us with a promise
That we all are sure is true.
His time and ours are different
But we know that he is due.

We'll no longer need the sun,
For our master brings the light.
Then the gate will be opened
With awe-inspiring might.

All hunger will be banished,
We will feast there by his seat.
His voice, the sound of music,
As we worship at his feet.

Forgiven indiscretions,
We in our youth committed,
With love he has forgotten
And we will be admitted.

With so much unmeasured love,
He's prepared for us a place.
There'll be joy we can't control
When we gaze upon his face.

And now the master's coming.
Hear his trumpet fill the air?
All worries are forgotten,
He's erased our every care.

Harry's wife says, "Must you honk
Every time we've been away?
It irritates the neighbors;
You should hear what they all say.

When you honk your horn like that,
Your dogs raise an awful din.
Hurry, open up the door;
Let your stupid mutts come in!"

Homecoming

Don't get upset with me like Ruth did, at least not until you've read the reasoning behind *Homecoming*. All too often we attempt to apply human values to God's plan for mankind. We insignificant humans can no more comprehend the thoughts and mind of God, than can the pets in this poem comprehend the daily activities of their master. If we approach our concept of God with this fact in mind, we will see how wrong it is for us to demand answers to every one of God's mysteries. Someone once said that humans are as ants in the sight of God. I know that God loves us more than I love ants, but the comparison probably gives humans the benefit of the doubt. The whole point that I want to make, in *Homecoming*, is that it would be just as futile for God to try and explain His actions to us, as it would be for us to try to explain our actions to our pets. Ruth's poodle thinks that I am God and I'm not going to tell her any different.

HOW ABOUT YOU?

It seems to me some people go
To church for conversation.
But lots of people that I know,
Go there for observation.
A few have found it quite the place
To get some rest and nod.
It makes you wonder just how many
Go there to worship God.

How About You

Having grown up attending church, I can see a vivid picture in my mind of people who fit each and every one of the lines in How About You. It's always fun to have a poem of this type to add a little humor to church bulletins and such. Unlike some other authors, I have no objection to your using my poems in church literature. It is common courtesy however, to give credit to the author for the selections you choose.

JUST A PENNY

Just a penny, just a penny,
The tramp saw it half-hidden there.
For such a small amount as that,
The tramp had given little care.

A little urchin saw it next
And wrapped it in his grimy fist.
He thought of wonders he would buy,
And he had dreamed of quite a list.

He took it in a candy store,
His newly found little penny.
He looked for things that he could buy
But found that there weren't any.

He tossed it down in childish rage,
He didn't think it was funny.
It wouldn't buy things he wanted
So to him it wasn't money.

A merchant bent to pick it up,
Half hidden there in all the dust.
Seeing it was just a penny,
He threw the coin down in disgust.

A widow lady found it next
But to her it seemed a treasure.
The value of a lone penny
Depends much on how you measure.

The coin became her total wealth,
The only money that she had.
The thought of how she'd use this coin
Had made the widow's heart grow glad.

That day at church a rich man gave
Ten thousand times the widow's mite.
But hers was much the greater gift
That day, in Jesus' loving sight.

Just A Penny

A penny is not worth a lot unless you're one penny short at the checkout counter. In *Just A Penny*, neither the boy, the beggar, nor the merchant saw any intrinsic value in the little tarnished penny. Only the widow was happy to find it. She was on her way to church and had nothing to put in the offering. In Mark 12:43, Jesus told his disciples, at the temple, that the widow who gave her two mites had given more than all of the rest. The two mites might not buy much in the way of earthly goods but it stored up treasures in Heaven for the widow.

Mark 12:42
Luke 21:2

A NOTE FROM JESUS

She received the note quite early,
It had come in the morning mail.
She had been living on welfare
And her health had become quite frail.

What the note said gave her new life.
"This evening I'll be passing through
And if it's not too much trouble
I would like to visit with you."

She quickly went to her closet
To put on her only nice dress.
The note that caused her excitement
Had been signed by Jesus, no less.

She had no food fit for Jesus...
On a piece of paper, she wrote,
"I've gone to the store, be right back."
And put on her only warm coat.

A loaf of bread and some cold cuts,
Took all of the money she had.
Wishing she had more for Jesus,
She hoped that He wouldn't feel bad.

She thought of how she must hurry,
Not wanting to make Jesus wait.
That's when she saw the poor beggar
On the street in front of her gate.

He asked, "Can you spare some money?"
For days I've had nothing to eat.
His clothes were tattered and ragged,
Old shoes barely covered his feet.

She gave him the food bought for Jesus,
There was nothing else she could do.
Because the poor man was shaking
She gave him her only coat too.

She worried, waiting for Jesus,
Had she missed Him while at the store?
She went to check on the beggar
And noticed a note on her door.

It was a thank-you from Jesus.
"It was really so nice to see you,
The cold cuts were most delicious,
The coat was a perfect fit too."

A Note from Jesus

Hebrews 13:12 tells you not to forget to entertain strangers because you may be entertaining angels unaware. One little girl asked her Sunday school teacher why the angels would be in their underwear. We have all read stories, and maybe you have had your own personnel experience, of angels helping during times of dire need. One of the most famous such visits, in the Bible, was when Abraham entertained three strangers, one of which was evidently the Lord. He had a feast prepared for them; the Lord promised him a son and that he would father a great nation. The Bible makes it clear, however, that angels don't always come in the form of helpers. They quite often come as ones in need to test your Christian love and generosity. One's willingness to offer help to someone shouldn't be predicated on how nice they look or how clean they are. If we were only sent beautiful, loving, people to help, it wouldn't be much of a test. It's our Christian duty to be ever watchful and ready to entertain the angels we encounter, even if they are in their underwear.

TWO TREES

God planted two trees in the garden,
One was, The Tree of Eternal Life.
Eve chose the other, Worldly Knowledge,
Which resulted in her pain and strife.

One tree in God's heavenly garden
Would have granted immortality.
The other, Tree of Worldly Knowledge,
Great suffering for humanity.

Eve's temptation was to be God-like,
Enticed by the Devil's hypnotic voice...
Which necessitates that you and I
Must be given the exact same choice.

We, too, can follow Satan's advice
And choose the world, as did Adam's wife,
Or we can choose the Son's redemption
Which guarantees us eternal life.

Two Trees

You would be surprised to know how many people think that there was only one tree to which the Bible gave special mention in the creation story. Perhaps you are one of them. We don't know why Adam and Eve had never tried the fruit of the Tree of Life, but it was such a wonderful tree that, after their downfall, God banned them from the garden, for fear that they would eat its fruit and live forever. What wonderful opportunities they missed by eating from the wrong tree. Most theologians believe that the Tree of Knowledge of Good and Evil was symbolic, as was the fruit. I have heard all kinds of ideas as to what the actual sin was, that first Eve and then Adam, committed. But I don't think that I have ever heard any opinions on what they might have done, that could give them the ability to live forever. If the fruit that caused their downfall was called, "Forbidden Fruit," what was the fruit called that would have given them immortality? And had God originally planned for them to partake of it and live forever? The choice of the two trees has been passed down to us and we also must choose of which tree we want to partake.

Genesis 2:9, 3:22

89

THE LESSON

Well, God let me down it was so plain to see,
It felt just the same as if He had kicked me.
I knew that the job was the one that I needed.
I told God my plan and I prayed and I pleaded.

My goal was in sight, my future planned out.
I knew what I needed, in my heart was no doubt.
So why did He do it? Why didn't He see?
Not getting that job would devastate me.

I told God right then, if he loved me so,
Then give me a reason. What didn't I know?
I was sorry for me, for I felt so blue.
I moped the day long with nothing to do.

I took my dog Spot to the park for a run.
Some kids had a ball, they were throwing for fun.
When I unhooked his leash to let Spot run free,
The kids threw the ball and it went right past me.

A truck I saw coming, so fast down the road,
No way he could stop, he had quite a load.
I, from my place, could see it all clearly.
I would lose Spot, the dog I loved dearly.

But Spot's only thought was the ball in the street,
Where he and the truck most surely would meet.
No time to cry out for he wouldn't hear,
His goal was the ball without caution or fear.

I stood by the curb and as he went by,
I kicked him so hard, he let out a cry.
The truck went on past. The ball was squashed flat.
I knelt down by Spot and gave him a pat.

I know that my kick was a hurtful surprise,
For Spot looked at me with questioning eyes.
I no longer saw God's will through a fog,
When I heard him ask, "Why did you kick your dog?"

91

The Lesson

God has a plan for each of our lives. It is just as impossible for us to understand that plan, as it was for the dog in this poem, to understand why his master kicked him. Some of us can look back at times when we felt like God was ignoring our prayers and see how it worked out for the best. Others, like Spot, will never know why and how God has protected them. Sometimes being kicked isn't all that bad when we consider the alternative.

THE LOST SHEEP

I knew that things were wrong with life.
I lost my job and lost my wife.

From deep within there came a voice,
"It's time for you to make a choice."

No easy thing for me to do.
I gave up God at twenty-two.

I used the paper for my search.
I had to find a godly church.

The ad was good, it sounded true,
"Come let us share our love with you."

They shook my hand at the front door
And then they spoke to me no more.

"Fill out this card and sign your name."
I sat there with my heart aflame.

"It's just to count the ones who're new.
We promise we won't bother you."

No one really seemed to care,
How much, right then, I needed prayer.

A keyboard loud, with sound of chimes.
They sang one song a thousand times.

They spoke of giving without limits.
The offering took a hundred minutes.

The worship then, sincere and loud,
It was a very joyful crowd.

A "Just-For-Christians" altar call,
I didn't fit in here at all.

No call for me to yield my soul,
No call for me to join the fold.

When all the Christians went to pray,
I quietly stood and slipped away.

Lost Sheep

So often we get caught up in our own relationship with God, family, or anything else, that we forget God's great commission, which is to take His Word to those who don't know Him. I saw this happen at our church one Sunday morning. When I got home I wrote *Lost Sheep.* Several of us shook his hand as he left and mouthed the words, "Glad to have you" and "Be sure to come back", but maybe he had come for something more. Perhaps he had a special need for prayer or was he just passing through? Did we miss a chance to make him feel at home and perhaps to add another member to our congregation? Maybe the church office will use his visitor's card to follow up, maybe the chance is gone forever. Have you ever seen this happen in your church? Maybe it has even happened to you, I hope not.

Matthew 18:12

WIDOW'S MITE

Jesus saw her at the temple
The day she tithed her widow's mite.
She has survived down through the ages,
Though she's usually out of sight.

Today she depends on welfare,
Not quite enough to make ends meet.
And some months she has to decide,
should she buy medicine or eat.

But she will always honor God
And she tithes her meager wages,
Just the same as those before her
Always did, down through the ages.

Maggie is just such a woman
And Jesus is her faithful friend.
If she fails to tithe her welfare,
She is certain her life will end.

Once when pastor came to visit,
She said she had just gotten up.
"I'm having some tea for breakfast,
Wouldn't you like to have a cup?"

The pastor took a sip and thought,
"Her memory's getting shorter."
He said, "Maggie this isn't tea,
This cup's only filled with water."

She said, " Now isn't Jesus good?
He's always a blessing to me.
I know it is only water
But Jesus makes it taste like tea!"

The Widow's Mite

One of the stories that we learned in Sunday school was the *Widow's Mite*. Jesus was deeply touched, that day in the temple, by the widow's generosity. He used her offering as an example to his disciples. One doesn't have to be of the Christian faith to learn from Jesus' teaching. Of course the moral of the story is to make the most of what you have. In my version of that old story, the widow shares her tea (which is only water) with her pastor. But more importantly, she shares her faith that it will also taste like tea to him. *Just a Penny*, on page 84, is a different version of the widow's mite. It is such a good story I might write more.

Mark 12: 42-43

MISDIRECTION

It was up to God to show me
Just how I was to live my life,
To reveal to me my purpose
And show me who would be my wife.

For hadn't he fed Elijah
And all those people on the mount?
I knew that he would care for me
If my life was going to count.

I would never beg for money
Like all those preachers on TV.
But I would teach the multitudes,
The ones that God would send to me.

And then, one day I heard God's voice,
It came to me out of the blue.
He told me where I was to go
And told me just what I should do.

So I boxed a few belongings
And went far out into the woods.
I would serve God as a teacher
And have no need for earthly goods.

First, I made a lean-to shelter
And just sat down upon my box.
When, on the path, I saw movement.
It was a little crippled fox.

Back in the trees I heard a noise,
Then there emerged a large black bear.
He brought a rabbit to the fox,
Walked off, and left it lying there.

Was this God's way to let me know
Just what he meant for me to be?
This tiny little crippled fox,
Is that the way that God saw me?

Next day I watched the little fox
As he, once more, lay by his den.
And then the bear came from the trees
And fed the little fox again.

Then I knew this was the lesson
That God had wanted me to see.
So I sat down and I waited
For someone to come and feed me.

Two days and nights I waited there.
I was in a terrible mood.
If I'm to be God's crippled fox,
Then who's supposed to bring me food?

Again I heard the voice of God,
It came while I was musing there.
"You weren't supposed to be my fox,
I wanted you to be my bear."

Misdirection

This is a poem about selective misunderstanding. It's something we all learned to do as kids. How many times did we say, "But Mom, I thought you said ....(It has been said that "Mom" is the only one syllable English word that your teenager can say in three syllables). Here we have a man who wants to dedicate his whole life to teaching God's word. In exchange he wanted God to meet and answer all of his challenges, the first being a constant food supply. It was easy for him to assume that the fox was to be his example. How about you? Are you a fox, or a bear?

NEGLECTED

Pastor was coming,
Now what should we do?
Where did we put it?
Not one of us knew.

We frantically looked;
We searched high and low.
It had to be somewhere,
Just where did it go?

The whole family's searched.
It's somewhere around.
Before he gets here,
It's got to be found.

He hasn't been here
Since last New Year's Day.
Did something we do
Keep Pastor away?

It's Christmas again,
We put up our tree.
All decorated
For Pastor to see.

Perhaps he'd not notice
That it wasn't there.
It seemed to have vanished,
Like they say, in thin air.

The preacher had come
And gone on his way.
He may not have noticed,
He sure didn't say.

We got out the box,
Not seen for a year.
More decorations
We all held so dear.

We opened the box
We'd packed with such care,
That's when we found it...
Our Bible was there.

When next we have need
For our Holy Book,
It's in the same box
So we'll know where to look.

Neglected

Do you know where yours is? I hope that this poem isn't about your family. Bibles aren't made to be put out on the coffee table for everyone to see. They are supposed to be used daily. One grandfather left a hundred dollar bill in his son's family Bible. When he visited a year later, it was still there. Every member of the family should have a Bible and be encouraged to use it daily. The preacher probably didn't leave because he didn't see a Bible; he probably left because he could tell that he was making them feel uncomfortable.

THE NIGHT CLERK

When I was born, the mid-wife said
That one day I'd change history.
Now what she meant has always been,
To all of us, a mystery.

My parents had been way too poor
To send me off somewhere to school,
But they taught me to be honest
And to obey the golden rule.

They taught me what was right and wrong
And the way I should treat others.
They said to just treat everyone
As if they were all my brothers.

And when we said our prayers each night,
They always told me that they knew
That what the mid-wife said of me,
Would turn out, someday, to be true.

And with parental pride they bragged
That I was doing very well,
When I got a job as night clerk
In this old second-rate hotel.

I have a place to sleep each day
And all the food I eat is free.
But the job is such a dead end,
There is no future here for me.

If I can't find a better one,
I think I'll be here 'til I'm dead.
The only thing that I will change
Will be the sheets on every bed.

No one would stay in this old dump
Unless their budget's awfully tight.
Our building needs a lot of work,
It's not a very pretty sight.

Just the unimportant stay here.
We're not the best hotel in town.
The Hilton Hotel on Main Street
Is where the rich are always found.

And if I'm going to change things,
They are the ones I need to meet.
Just one guest that is important
Would surely be a welcomed treat.

Soon, a lot of guests will be here,
To pay their taxes in our town
And everybody is coming
From all the places close around.

There're so many reservations,
I'm sure we won't have space enough.
The owner said he'd need my room
And told me I should move my stuff.

Now, I tried to be sarcastic
Because I didn't give a darn,
So I asked if he intended
To put me outside in the barn!

I guess that I was kind of dumb,
I know that I won't try it twice,
But once I moved the two cows out,
I fixed the place up really nice.

I used some hay that smelled real fresh
To make myself a kind of bed
In the extra wooden manger
Where the cows are usually fed.

I couldn't take a lot of time
Or I might have been in trouble.
With so many people coming,
Everyone was working double.

The better rooms were first to go,
They really filled up very fast.
Then all the other rooms were full,
The halls and lobby filled up last.

Then when all the guests were sleeping,
And it was quiet as a tomb,
There came a voice from behind me,
Saying, "Good sir, we need a room".

Now the man was tired and haggard
Like one who bore a heavy load,
But his wife was young and pretty
With a sweet face that kind of glowed.

Though the husband tried to hide it,
On his face was a look of fear,
For his lovely wife was pregnant
And one could tell her time was near.

Well, there was no room in the Inn
But they both looked so cold and tired,
I knew I would have to help them
Even though it could get me fired.

Every space in the inn was filled
With all the people we could cram,
And every other inn was full
In the whole town of Bethlehem.

But my own space, out in the barn,
That I fixed up, belonged to me,
So I could let Mister Joseph
And his wife Mary have it free.

Then, with no place for me to sleep,
I thought about my mystery.
How could somebody such as I
Have hope of changing history?

The Night Clerk

If all of the inns were filled that night in Bethlehem, then there must have been inns. If there were inns, then there must have been night clerks. One certain night clerk that night, two thousand years ago, could have gotten his name recorded in history. Instead, we will never know just who let Mary and Joseph use their stable. The poem is, of course, tongue in cheek. People who don't understand my humor are always pointing out that I am mixing modern times with Biblical times. Don't let that throw you, just enjoy the poem.

EXPIRATION DATE

People think that things have changed
Since the Holy Book was written.
They say that God has changed his mind
Since His only Son was smitten.

They say that hell is just a myth
Because their God is much too kind.
To justify their favorite sin,
They claim the Scripture's mis-defined.

Some try to change the Holy Text
To soothe troubled conscience questions.
Convinced the Scriptures' Ten Commandments
Are really, only Ten Suggestions.

To keep up with the modern times,
The laws once carved in solid stone
Can, as of now, all be ignored,
With sins no longer to atone.

The Scripture calls these people fools,
Who wager their eternal fate.
I've checked the Bible through and through,
It has no expiration date!

Expiration Date

Nowadays we have a lot of denominations telling us that what we read in the Bible is not necessarily what God meant. They say that things are different in our modern day and that a loving God would certainly change with modern society's needs. My Bible says that God does not change, that he is the same yesterday, today and forever. Those who write their own interpretation of the Bible, changing God's gender or the sexual orientation of some of the Bible's most loved characters, are certainly not divinely inspired. They ignore the warning God gives us in Revelations, 22:18. God's food for our souls, unlike food for our bodies, has no expiration date.

OPEN HOUSE SURGERY

I invited Jesus
To come live in my heart.
I would give Him a tour,
Just to make a good start.

I was proud of my heart,
As I showed Him around.
I had thought it was strong
And it's foundation sound.

But, in the library,
I could tell by His looks,
That He didn't approve
Of some of my books.

Then the living room too,
Was not quite up to par.
He wasn't too happy
That it still had a bar.

My bathroom was spotless.
He could see it was clean
Except I'd forgotten
Just that one magazine.

And then, in the guest room,
There was something I missed;
Some questionable friends
I had kept on the list.

With my heart still so full
Of so much worldly stuff,
Would He want to live there?
Was my heart good enough?

I sure wanted Him there,
To give my life meaning.
He said, "Invite me in,
I'll help with the cleaning."

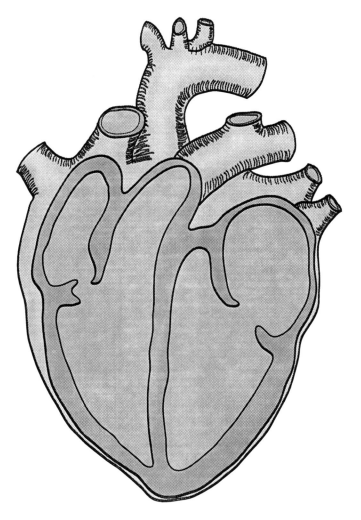

Open House Surgery

In this day and time, you can go into the hospital, have open-heart surgery and be home in time to watch the evening news. The procedure may no longer be called "open heart surgery" but in the past, to accomplish the same task, would have required cracking your chest and cutting into your heart. Of course none of these procedures can be done without your permission. Salvation works on the same principle. God will not invade your heart without your permission. Also, as in heart surgery, the procedure was updated and made quite simple by the death of Jesus on the cross.

PETTY CASH

He was a tax collector,
The very best of the best,
For he collected taxes
Overlooked by all the rest.

So, just why should he report
All the tax he collected?
The coins he kept for himself
Would never be detected.

One night a thief found the coins,
A right goodly pile of loot,
In the back of a closet,
In the tax collector's boot.

He didn't mean to kill him,
At least not to kill him then,
Because he planned to come back
And to rob him once again.

Now the thief was of the kind
Who would always like to brag.
He talked about the silver
That he carried in his bag.

Well it didn't take too long
For the thief to meet his fate.
He realized his mistake
Just a little bit too late.

If you cheat when you gamble,
One thing you should never do,
Is to gamble with people
That are much meaner than you.

Now the coin sack's new owner
Knew naught of its history.
But to all of those who knew,
His death was no mystery.

Not a one of them would touch
The gamblers ill-gotten gain,
They just left him by the road,
On his back, out in the rain.

A passing priest who saw him
Was disgusted at the sight.
And the priest thought to himself,
That fate had served this man right.

Then a traveler called out,
"This poor fellow needs a priest.
Can't you see that he's dying?
Won't you comfort him at least?"

Just then, the priest saw the coins,
Enough to pay for his plan.
So, of course, the priest would help
This poor, wretched, dying, man!

Then he quickly slid the coins
Down inside his garment's hem.
And then, with practiced fingers,
He skillfully counted them.

There were thirty little coins
Of silver, so very bright.
They would pay for the evil
He had planned that very night.

He hurried to the temple
To tell all his friends the news.
How God had just provided
Thirty coins that they could use.

"I hope that there is plenty,
He's the greedy kind I fear.
That's him over by the door.
Hey Judas, come over here."

Petty Cash

Did you ever wonder where the money came from, that was paid to Judas, to betray Jesus,? Was it some tithes-payer's money, who had given his tenth to the temple to be used for God's work? Maybe it was made up of a bunch of widows' mites. I would rather think that it was tainted money from the beginning. *Petty Cash* is a poem that tells a story about where the 'thirty pieces of silver' might have originated. This is my version of the story and I'm sticking to it.

Matthew 26:15

PRIORITIES

Oh, he wanted to go but he didn't have time.
After all, not to go, was it such a crime?
His intentions were good, when he promised to go,
But at the last minute he would always say, "No".

And God wouldn't notice, from his lofty perch,
If one single person never had time for church.
He knew not to go was most surely a sin
But he joked, if he went, the roof would cave in.

He met a young lady he wanted for wife;
He promised he'd change with more time for life.
The wedding was short, in front of a judge.
She opted for church but he wouldn't budge.

He said he would go when the kids came along.
She'd heard that before, his usual old song.
She knew that this promise, like the one long before,
Had intentions so good but not a lot more.

"The time is not right", is what he would say,
When she went to church and he went to play.
He never attended an after church mingle.
Church friends, of his wife, all thought she was single.

Their kids were all part of the church Christmas play.
They asked him to go, but he would just say,
His usual verse, with a wink and a grin,
"If I went to church, the roof would fall in".

He told everyone he intended to go
But with time so important, he'd have to say, "No".
His kids were all grown and had gone their own way,
Still church had no place in his Sabbath Day.

It happened so fast that time had no part.
They said it was stress that weakened his heart.
Now he couldn't use his usual verse,
When they took him to church, in a shiny black hearse.

Priorities

People often ask me where the ideas for my poems come from. I travel about seventy miles to visit my dentist. That's because the Veterans Administration gives me free dental care. One day, while driving home, I noticed a bumper sticker that said, "Don't visit church for the first time in a hearse". By the time I had completed the two-hour trip home, I had *Priorities* pretty well written in my head. I wanted to word it in such a way that it would emphasize how we so often place the priorities of this life above those that could influence our relationship with God and our fate in eternity. If you have a friend who gives you the old 'roof will fall in' story, give him a copy of *Priorities*.

RAIN

Rain falls on the just and the unjust.
Today, a very unjust fella
Made sure it fell only on the just,
When he walked off with my umbrella!

Rain

There are many quotations that are falsely attributed to the Bible. Some of them are pretty gross. Two of the ones that can be mentioned, in a family oriented book, are the one about cleanliness being next to godliness and the one that claims that God works in mysterious ways, His wonders to perform. There are people who will argue with you, until they are blue in the face, that their favorite quotation is in the Bible. Once in Vietnam, I corrected a young sergeant who was quoting a particular offensive "scripture" to justify his off base dalliances. He was so sure he was right, that after spending a whole night searching for it in a borrowed Bible, he went to a chaplain for help. The chaplain agreed with him and claimed that he had used the scripture in a paper he had written in Bible School. He bet me a steak dinner. The bet got spread from building to building and soon you could walk in any office and see men thumbing through their Bibles. It was before the day of computerized Bibles so the good outcome was that a whole lot of Bible study went on. I never got my steak dinner because, even though he couldn't find the scripture, the chaplain insisted that he knew it was in there. I said all of this to point out that even though I have been told it is a bogus scripture, the quotation about rain on the just and the unjust is factual, Matt 5:45. "Spare the rod and spoil the child," is another bogus quotation however it is based on scripture, Prov. 13:24. My wife's brother, in an attempt to avoid a spanking, once changed the quotation around a bit and told his mother that the Bible says that you should spare the rod and spoil the child. The quotation, "Spare the rod and spoil the child," is actually from a poem by Samuel Butler, written back in the eighteen hundreds.

Matt. 5:45

THE ROSE

It was in a used bookstore,
In a book he'd gone to buy,
The comments he read, in the margins,
Would put tears in a cynical eye.

In lines any author would envy,
She had penned her concepts of life.
Her words showed such inner beauty,
They cut through his heart like a knife.

He vowed he would find this woman
Whose writing still burned in his heart.
But how could he keep such a vow,
He didn't know where he should start.

In the margin, on one of the pages,
He found his first tiny clue.
In a line, she referred to herself
And said that her nickname was Brew.

And then, on the very last page,
The name and address of a friend.
He sent her his heart in a letter,
How he'd found the lines she had penned.

With a kiss and a prayer he had mailed it,
His chances were slim he well knew.
He wrote on the back of the envelope,
"Will you forward this letter to Brew?"

It was then fate dealt him a blow
That the Devil himself must have crafted.
A government telegram came,
With a notice that he had been drafted.

A whole year of training and moving,
Then a letter had reached him in 'Nam.
From her, the girl in the margin,
Forwarded there to him by his mom.

No lines that he could concoct
Could match what she wrote to him.
It filled his whole day with joy
Which no war or fighting could dim.

They wrote back and forth to each other,
'Til each knew the other by heart.
She insisted that looks didn't matter,
No pictures exchanged from the start.

The comfort they felt with each other,
Their thoughts in perfect coherence;
A love that they both agreed
Transcended all personal appearance.

Then his enlistment was over.
If his heart could withstand the strain,
They would meet in Grand Central station,
Where she would arrive by train.

Just how would he know his beloved
With crowds of people so great?
"No picture," she still insisted,
"Just be there and don't be late."

He asked what she would be wearing,
"Just tell me what color your clothes."
She said they would know in their hearts
and she would be carrying a rose.

He arrived there two hours early,
This is the day they would meet.
So long he'd dreamed of this day
With plans just how they would greet.

He knew her the second he saw her,
Perfection from head to her toes.
His heart, overwhelmed by her beauty,
But where had she hidden the rose?

Her perfume engulfed him in passing,
Her countenance bouncy and gay.
He knew he was smitten forever,
When she whispered, "Going my way?"

It was then that he saw the woman
Watching them in quizzical pose;
No beauty, but eyes that showed depth,
And she was holding a rose!

His anguish a burden too great,
His vision was walking away.
But the love he had shared with this woman,
No doubt where his future lay.

With feet like lead, he approached her
To take her in his embrace.
"Soldier, I don't think I know you!"
But a smile was crossing her face.

"The girl who just passed you by,
Asked that I give this to you.
She said she would wait in the lobby
And that you would know what to do."

"She said no love could be greater
And told me just how she knows,
Your souls were meant for each other.
She knew you would bring her this rose."

The Rose

This was my first love poem. The story on which it is based, was sent to us by a friend; best of all, it came just in time for Valentine's Day. Ruth sent the poem out in her Valentines and I was overwhelmed by the responses. I hope that you get just as much enjoyment out of reading *The Rose*. It always seems to me that stories improve when put to rhyme. Maybe it's just because so much thought has to be put into each line to carry out the rhythm and make the necessary words rhyme. As I see it, the moral of the story is to follow your heart but take care of your commitments first. If our hero had followed his dream girl without the rose to give to her, he would not have measured up to her expectations though he still may have won her in the end.

GOD'S DRESS CODE

Everyone had noticed the stranger
Coming into their church off the street.
Not quite the quality of person
Most of them had occasion to meet.

His clothing was so very common
With his faded jeans and unshined shoes.
He was not the kind of a person
That should occupy one of their pews.

He sat there alone before service
And no one came over to greet him.
No one offered him a songbook,
No deacon came over to meet him.

And then when the service was over,
And the stranger was starting to leave,
The pastor walked over beside him
Placing his hand on the stranger's sleeve.

He said, "I can tell you're a Christian
And that you are no stranger to prayer.
If you plan to come back to our church,
Ask Jesus what he thinks you should wear."

The next Sunday the stranger came back,
His clothes and appearance still the same.
No effort to make an improvement,
Showing no sign of remorse or shame.

Pastor asked, "Did you talk to Jesus?
Did you ask Jesus what you should wear?
You haven't improved your appearance,
Do you think that our God doesn't care?"

Then the stranger said to the pastor,
Who was standing there blocking the door,
"Jesus said that he couldn't help me
Because he'd never been here before."

God's Dress Code

God's Dress Code was derived from a story sent to me by a missionary in China. Of course I changed the story all around to be able to make it rhyme. Christians too often attempt to make new converts into carbon copies of themselves. I mentioned earlier in the book that early missionaries in tropical climates found that it was better to teach God's love and the plan of salvation first, before trying to get the new converts dressed. We have a friend who was a native of Pitcairn Island. She said that as a teenager, she thought it quite wicked to sneak over to a part of the island that the Seventh Day Adventists missionaries never visited and pig out on lobster. The missionaries never quite convinced her that eating shellfish was a sin. Then there is the story about the missionary who told a newly converted tribal chief that he must have only one wife. The chief agreed on the condition that the missionary be the one to tell his second wife's father, who was a most feared leader of a neighboring tribe. The missionary decided that God was big enough to forgive the convert of such a small sin.

SAPLING

While clearing brush the other day,
I came upon a little tree.
For such a sapling it was tall
But was much too thin and spindly.

It was wrapped tight with thorny vines
And scrub and brush grew close around.
I would try to clear around it
And save the little tree I'd found.

The thorny vines gave it support;
But what an awful price to pay,
For they would stop all outward growth
And choke its very life away.

The shrubs and brush, that pushed up close,
Had kept the little tree from light.
No blowing wind to strengthen growth,
It had become a spindly sight.

The brush I cut from close around,
I quickly cast upon a fire.
I tried to pull the vines away
But they had grown as tough as wire.

So deep imbedded they'd become;
The ugly thorns resisted me.
They tore my flesh and brought the blood
As I removed them from the tree.

Then it was left all by itself,
This lovely little tree I'd found.
But by itself, it could not stand
And it bent low down to the ground.

Destined to be a mighty oak,
It bowed down low in front of me,
Now only I could guide its growth
And save this little spindly tree.

Just like that tree our children are,
If we don't guide what friends they choose.
The ones in life we hold most dear,
We can so very quickly lose.

The thorns of life more quickly wrap,
Than those on that small spindly tree.
The things that shape our children's lives
Are what they learn from you and me.

Sapling

My fish farm partner, Alan Rudd, and I were clearing brush behind one of the lake dams when we found a little post oak sapling that we decided to save. It was rather small in diameter for its height and when we finally got all of the yaupons and green brier cleared away from it, we found that it was too weak to stand on its own. It had been depending on the vines and brush around it, to give it support. It was further weakened by the loss of nutrients that the more hardy brush pulled from the soil in which its roots grew and from the lack of sunlight, which was blocked out by the larger plants. We had to prop it up with sticks until it was able to grow strong enough to stand on its own. When I grow tomato seedlings inside my greenhouse, where they are not exposed to wind, I daily brush my hand across the tops of them and they respond by growing thicker, stronger stems. If parents want to "train up a child in the way he should go," as Solomon suggested, then they mustn't allow him to receive his training from questionable sources as the little sapling did.

Prov. 22:6

SELECTIVE CHOICE

The Government says the land is yours
But you're not allowed to use it.
There's a tiny snail that lives there
And they can't let you abuse it.

The Government says the trees are yours
But it won't let you cut them down.
There's a small bird that uses them
So all your trees are hallowed ground.

The Government says that it's your swamp
But you're not allowed to drain it.
A small fish is in need of it
And it's your job to maintain it.

The Government says that it's your field
But you're not allowed to till it.
A little mouse has been seen there,
It's possible you might kill it.

The Government says the water's yours,
To sprout your crops and quench their thirst,
But then they came and turned it off,
There's life downstream and it comes first.

The woman says, "THIS BODY IS MINE,"
But God put a wee life there.
The Government says, "Just kill it."
And no one seems at all to care!

Selective Choice

I once asked a woman, who referred to herself as pro-choice, if she thought that it was alright to end a one-day-old baby's life. She said, "Of course not!" So I asked her what about the day before it was born? She was still uncomfortable with that. I kept backing it up until she said that she wasn't going to play my game any more. A Christian who claims to be in favor of abortion is not well versed in the Bible. I am sure that they would have a struggle with their conscience if they ever actually watched a fully formed young human, being brutally killed by what they refer to as a late term abortion technique. In this poem, I am pointing out the fact that trees and animals are given more protection, by our laws, than unborn babies.

PAID IN FULL

The Heavenly Court was packed,
The angel jury there.
As God would be my judge
What hope that He'd be fair?

For I had not been perfect,
That I had strayed was true.
The court appointed lawyer,
Would he know what to do?

Judge God said I had chosen
This lawyer long ago.
My chance of making Heaven
Without him, worse than low.

The prosecution gathered;
I felt waves of doom.
The team was led by Satan,
Whose evil filled the room.

Just then my lawyer entered
And I saw Satan blench.
He said, "Judge God, Your Honor,
May I approach the bench?"

He couldn't hide his anger,
His whispers' evil hiss.
I heard him ask Judge God,
"What trickery is this?"

"You know this man is guilty,
Much evil he has done.
How can this trial be fair?
The lawyer is your son!"

God said, "You are aware,
I promised long ago,
This lawyer is available
To everyone, you know."

The Devil then showed panic,
He threatened an appeal.
God said, "There's no higher court
And you can't cut a deal."

"The lawyer is my only Son,
He gave His life for this;
For those who will accept His help
There's no way they can miss."

I wondered how I could afford
A lawyer with such pull.
But when he handed me my bill,
On it was written, "PAID IN FULL."

Paid In Full

Paid In Full is based on a story that came over e-mail. I get a lot of good ideas that way. I just think that it makes them a lot more interesting when they are put to rhyme. I have been hard on lawyers in some of my poems, so it was a pleasant change to portray Jesus as our defense lawyer, in God's court of judgment. Jesus is one lawyer that anyone can afford, and no one can afford to be without; His terms are reasonable and He has never lost a case.

NO HOPE

I hope and pray
There is no God,
That life will end
Beneath the sod.

"You are a fool",
My friends all say
And then they ask
To whom I pray.

They make me seem
Like such a dope;
So I won't pray,
I'll only hope.

But there's no hope,
I start to see,
Without a God
How can there be?

No Hope

A news magazine, that I read, quoted a rock star as saying that he hoped and prayed that there wasn't a god or he would be in a lot of trouble. I wondered just who you pray to if you don't believe in God. Also, where do you put your hope? This is just a short little poem to cause people to think. It is a good poem to include in your church bulletin from time to time.

DARK

One thing about Dark, that I've learned,
Is that it's very very fast.
And in a race with Dark, I know
That Light would surely come in last.

Now Light and Dark can't get along,
Light always seems to rule the day.
Dark lurks about in holes and caves;
But when night comes, Dark has its way.

So Light is banished from the night,
For it does not know how to hide.
Although the moon and stars above
Try valiantly to take its side.

And man has done his very best
To cause the fight to be unfair.
But Dark's so sure of victory,
It doesn't even seem to care.

Small children are Dark's strongest foes,
In every room the battle's drawn.
No matter how much dads complain,
Light switches are always left on.

Dark, I know, will finally win;
There can be very little doubt.
With utmost patience Dark will wait
Until the last light has gone out.

Dark

It's been said that the only people that have absolutely no fear of dark are the blind. Since they have never seen light they are not afraid of what dark hides. I didn't write *Dark* as an allegory about Christ, The Light of the World, I was simply pointing out a few differences between light and dark in the natural world. It wouldn't make much sense to close the blinds to keep the dark out, now would it? Dark is not an entity in itself. It can only exist in the absence of light, the same as cold is the absence of heat. Maybe that's another poem.

TALENT

Poor Grackle knew his voice was bad
And he had learned it very soon.
He was the only bird he knew
Who couldn't even make a tune.

Now Grackle really loved to sing
And serenade the morning sun.
When all the other birds had choir,
He tried to join right in the fun.

A melody so pure and grand,
He formed within his tiny head.
But, when he tried to sing his tune,
The other birds all squawked and fled!

So Grackle just sat quietly by,
His head beneath his little wing.
The only joy he got from life
Was when he heard the others sing.

One day the Wise Owl came to sit
Beside poor Grackle on his limb;
He asked him why he seemed so sad
And why his countenance so dim.

When Grackle told him of his plight
And that he'd vowed to sing no more,
The Wise Owl smiled, and then he said,
"Some birds can sing; that's what they're for."

"But silence, in the woods and fields,
Would surely be an awful thing
If just the ones with purest voice
Were the only birds allowed to sing."

Talent

Not everyone can carry a tune, I happen to be one of those who can't, as I am completely tone deaf. My singing sounds as good to me as anyone else's does, unfortunately no one shares my opinion. When my children were very young, they wouldn't go to sleep without my singing songs to them. We had our own family versions of all of the children's songs such as 'Jesus Loves Me' and 'Jesus Loves the Little Children.' (i.e. "Jesus loves the little children, all the children in this house, Ruthie, Ronny, Jonny, Tim, they are precious unto Him…") When I went to Vietnam for a year, I left a tape of my singing and it was worn out by the time I got home. Now they try to leave the room when I sing, 'Happy Birthday'! I don't know why God chose to make some of us grackles but you nightingales will just have to put up with us.

144

NO TIME TO PRAY

When I got up this morning,
I didn't have time to pray.
I had way too much to do
Just to finish in one day.

I had no time for breakfast,
Just some coffee on the run.
And no time for thanks to God
For the things that he had done.

Now when in such a hurry,
Why wouldn't my old car start?
The bad words I called that wreck,
I sure hope weren't from my heart.

And then when I got to work,
Of all the days they could pick,
Two people who I needed
Had already called in sick.

Things were to get no better,
Though working without a pause.
The project so important
Had become a long lost cause.

But tonight, when I asked God
Why he failed to ease my task,
God said he would have loved to,
Had I taken time to ask.

No Time To Pray

Before my dad went into business for himself, he was a contractor. He always tried to impress on me the importance of taking my time and doing it right the first time. He followed the old carpenter adage of measuring it twice and cutting it once. When we neglect an established routine on the behalf of speed, we often find that we have spent more time in the long run. Christians have found that the best way to start their day is to have a little talk with God and let him know the areas in which they will most probably need his help during the day. Just going over your plans with God will often give you new insight into your planned activities. It never does any good to say, "God why didn't you help me!" when you never asked for his help.

146

THE VINE

It was a tiny island,
Had just a tree or two.
That I was stranded there,
I was sure nobody knew.

The ship had sunk so fast,
The raft a God-sent gift.
And God had made the choice
For which way I would drift.

No water on the island,
The raft would catch a little.
If I left it out at night,
Dew puddled in the middle.

I gathered up some driftwood
And made myself a shelter.
My cistern raft, a roof,
For protection from the swelter.

A vine grew up beside it
And added to my shade.
For a simple cooking fire,
This world's riches I would trade.

Raw seafood is a meal
Of which you quickly tire.
Each night I prayed to God
That he would send me fire.

And then my lovely vine
Just shriveled up and died.
Self-pity overwhelmed me.
I sat right down and cried.

Right then I felt like Jonah
When God destroyed his vine.
For I was quick to question
Why God had not saved mine.

That night the dead dry leaves
Caught fire while I slept.
My raft, my shelter, all burned up.
I cursed God as I wept.

Was this some godly joke,
His answer to my prayer?
My fate was sealed for certain.
God didn't seem to care.

God's plan for me was obvious,
Now, I was going to die.
I couldn't understand it.
To me, God was a lie.

The boat came at first light,
My God was not a liar.
I asked how they had found me...
They had seen my signal fire!

The Vine

Everyone knows the story of Jonah and the whale but the story of Jonah and the gourd is not that well known. In both stories, God attempts to teach the same lesson to Jonah. You would think that getting swallowed by a whale would be lesson enough, but not for old Jonah.   Think back and be honest, how many times have you had to be hit on the head before it did more than make lumps? In this little poem our hero, like Jonah, thinks that he has God's plan for himself all worked out and that he understands it even better than God. All of my life I have heard the old saying, "The Lord giveth and the Lord taketh away." But the final verse of the saying should be that he will replace it with something much better if we will just let him. When your dreams catch on fire, check with God; it might just be a signal fire.

Jonah 4:6-7

WARM LOVE

Shirley was a timid child,
Such a ragged little waif.
She hung around the mission
Because that's where she felt safe.

Her parents let her wander,
They just didn't seem to care.
As long as they could claim her
When they went to draw welfare.

She lived in old Shantytown;
Just a bunch of makeshift shacks
Built out of crates and boxes,
Over by the railroad tracks.

She had a ragged dolly
That she carried everywhere.
Dolly was her constant friend
And she treated her with care.

It was the Christmas season,
The mission decorated
With the life-size manger scene
Its members had created.

The days and nights were frigid,
And just breathing hurt your nose.
The mission struggled daily
To furnish warm coats and clothes.

Their new manger scene drew crowds,
It became a source of pride.
Passers by stopped to leave gifts
In a box that was supplied.

That's why the pastor wondered
Who would desecrate the scene?
To put that thing with Jesus,
Why would someone be so mean?

Then he recognized the doll
That was in the baby's crib.
How could such a timid girl
Treat the manger scene so glib?

When he found the little girl,
In the mission, keeping warm,
He asked about the manger;
She said she had meant no harm.

"I had no gift for Jesus
Like the wise men did of old.
But I knew so very well
That the baby must be cold."

"So if the little baby
Can be Jesus, don't you see?
I thought it would be okay
For my dolly to be me."

"My gift to Baby Jesus
Is just me, to keep him warm.
I'm lying close beside him
And his head is on my arm."

"I no longer need my doll
Because Jesus is my friend.
We'll always be together,
We'll be friends until the end."

Then the pastor hurried back
And put Dolly in her place.
You could tell he had been touched,
By the teardrops on his face.

If you see a manger scene,
Way up north, where it is cold.
You may just find two babies,
At least that's what I've been told.

Warm Love

I wrote this poem several years ago so I no longer remember whether I heard the story from someone or if I made it up. Like in my poem, Baby Jesus, the preacher was too quick to pass judgment. The little girl was raised in the same type of surroundings that Jesus was born into. She had experienced cold and was willing to give her most treasured possession to Baby Jesus to keep him warm. The little girl's doll, like the widow's mite, was all that she had to offer.

THE WAVE

It started as a tiny ripple,
On its journey toward the distant shore.
It grew into a towering wave.
Its voice became a mighty roar.

With strength that knew no earthly bounds,
When fed by summer storm and tide;
The little ripple, now a wave,
Rushed on with ever growing pride.

Mighty ships caught in its path
Were crushed like tiny bathtub toys.
The birds on islands miles away
Were startled by its awesome noise.

It finally reached the sandy shore
And there it lost all strength and motion.
Just water flowing back to sea,
One tiny part of Mother Ocean.

The Wave

The Wave. like so many of my poems, is a parody. Most of us spend our whole life seeking power. From the lowly wife abuser to the man or woman who attains high office, the objective is to have power over as many others as possible. Of course there are those who have a legitimate desire to benefit humanity, but as is readily obvious in an election year, they are a rarity. The wave grows and absorbs more and more of its surroundings, as it moves across the surface of the ocean. Even the mighty whale dives deep, as it passes over, but once it makes landfall it quickly dissipates and becomes once more just another part of the ocean. In the military community, as an officer with an important position, I was treated with the utmost respect. But after I retired, and moved back into the rural community from whence I came, no one even knew what my military rank had been. It took some getting used to being called by my first name. The nice thing about the loss of power is that it comes with the loss of a lot of responsibility.

MANGER SCENE

It is Christmas time again
With the many manger scenes.
Both shepherds poor and wise men
Who were all of wealthy means.

The cattle are all healthy
And the donkey is well fed.
And little baby Jesus
Has a halo 'round his head.

Everything is so spotless,
Mary's clothes all look so clean.
It looks like they have just come
From a laundromat machine.

The scene is oh so cozy
With admirers gathered there.
The odor of Christmas trees
And fresh hay are in the air.

And on Joseph's face a smile,
Their future so bright and clear.
The wise men's gold for their tax
And soft Christmas tunes to hear.

God would pick a perfect place
For the birth of his one son,
An atmosphere filled with joy
And people all having fun.

The manger scenes that we buy,
And then view with such delight,
May not be too accurate
Of what happened late that night.

History says that Mary,
At the most, was just fifteen.
So there were really two babes
At that early manger scene.

The inn where they sought shelter,
At least as we have been told,
Was a bunch of empty stalls,
Uncomfortable, damp and cold

But even this stark shelter,
Denied to Jesus' mother;
All filled with early travelers,
They'd have to seek some other.

With no way to phone ahead
And certainly late at night.
All the inns already filled,
Irregardless of their plight.

A donkey, her limousine
On the day that she gave birth.
No beds with sheets and blankets,
With just straw to cover earth.

They finally found shelter,
Some say just a cold dank cave.
A place for feeding cattle
And with rats and mice to brave.

Some think the birth was easy
For God could have made it so,
And given an advantage,
Others moms would never know.

We know she had no doctor
And probably no midwife.
Had Joseph birthed a baby?
Never once in his whole life.

So now you get the picture,
It was not a pretty sight.
Our Savior born in the dark,
They had no electric light.

When at last the baby came,
Little time to count his toes.
He was cleaned as best they could
And then wrapped in swaddling clothes.

No friends there to gather 'round,
No one to send her flowers.
No parents to show her love,
Of course no baby showers.

He wore no paper diapers,
As a modern baby would.
No way to wash his clothing,
So he didn't smell so good.

The shepherds that gathered 'round
Were, for sure, a smelly lot
As they pushed close to Mary
Just to see the tiny tot.

The wise men, with their rich gifts,
Would not come 'til later years.
Mary had one special gift,
She had heard the angels' cheers.

But she had no time for rest,
To sleep late, or to relax.
They had to get up early,
To go pay their income tax.

So Jesus, used to splendor
That's unrivaled here on earth,
Was cast out in an instant
To a very lowly birth.

When you see the manger scene
That is spread beneath your tree,
Think about the sacrifice
Jesus made for you and me.

Manger Scene

Ruth handed me an article from a church magazine and said, "This would make a great poem." I had never stopped to think just how horrifying things must have been for the young mother, Mary, that night. Only a mother could imagine the misery of riding a donkey for days right up to the time of delivery. Think of Joseph's frustration. It was probably late at night when they arrived in Bethlehem and all of the inns were full. The only place he could find for his wife to give birth was a dark smelly cave that was used to shelter farm animals. Mary was probably already experiencing labor pains, as they neared Bethlehem, and Joseph had no idea where to turn for help. What kind of supplies had Mary packed in anticipation of the birth? At fifteen, how much did she know about what would be needed? Did Joseph even have a place to build a fire and warm some water? Having a baby while traveling today would be tough but Mary didn't have access to laundromats and disposable diapers. How often could she wash swaddling clothes in the cold of winter? Jesus was probably a stinky little baby. He could probably have used some of that frankincense and myrrh! I hope that I didn't ruin manger scenes for you altogether, but it probably wasn't the warm, clean, peaceful, romantic atmosphere we so often see portrayed.

THE WINDOW

Jack's bed was by the window
The whole time that they'd been there.
It really hadn't mattered;
Neither took the time to care.

Both of them were paralyzed
From the time they'd been in Nam.
They both had learned the hard way,
Of the deadly pop-up bomb.

Jack didn't like the TV
And visitors there were few,
So they lay and talked a lot,
There was nothing else to do.

Of the things they talked about,
One subject that was taboo;
Talk about their injuries
And the things they couldn't do.

Bill asked about the window
And the things that Jack could see.
Jack, quiet for a minute,
It might have been two or three.

Then Jack began to describe
All the things he saw outside,
The park, the pond and the ducks,
And the Shetland pony ride.

Their days became full again
With the wonders, Jack would tell.
Bill could almost taste the things
That the vendors came to sell.

He shared the love of couples,
Who were strolling through the park,
Holding hands beside the pond
Until daylight turned to dark.

Bill's dull life now full of sights
Seen vividly through Jack's eyes;
Children playing after school,
He could hear their joyful cries.

But he began to envy
All the sights that Jack could see.
Just to see them for himself,
How much better it would be.

Then it happened late one night,
Jack had a bad choking spell.
Bill could tell that Jack would die
If he didn't ring the bell.

He thought about the window
And how much he envied Jack.
A too late call, nurses came
But they couldn't bring Jack back.

Anticipation stole his sleep,
And a bit of conscience too,
He asked Nurse to move his bed
So that he could see the view.

A puzzled look crossed her face
But then quickly she complied.
At last the window was his
And he turned to look outside.

A brick wall was all he saw
And his heart began to race.
"Where is the park that Jack saw?"
He yelled in the nurse's face.

The nurse, startled by his tone,
Said with words a bit unkind,
"You lived with Jack all these months
And didn't know Jack was blind?"

The Window

One of my uncles, Tom Spurway, first told me this story many years ago. I brought it up to date a little by jumping ahead a couple of wars. I'm sure that it isn't true but it could be. There is certainly a good moral lesson in the poem. If you want something so badly that you will hurt others to get it, you may find out that what you get is much less than you expected and you just might ruin what you already have.

WOODEN BOWL

He was a sloppy eater
And he made a lot of noise.
He set a bad example
Before their two little boys.

Then one day he broke his plate
And it made them both quite mad.
They called him Bumbling Fool...
They both yelled that he was bad.

They sat him in a corner
And there he would eat his meals;
Where they could clean more easily,
All his messes and his spills.

They got him a wooden bowl
And they bought a wooden cup.
Things he couldn't quickly break
That were easy to clean up.

Through this awful sad ordeal,
Not one word did Grandpa say,
For he loved his two grandsons,
He would not be sent away.

Then one day, the two small boys
Brought in several scraps of wood.
The mother and the daddy
Watched the boys from where they stood.

"Just what are you guys making?"
The dad was the first to ask.
"From the looks of your endeavors,
It's quite a serious task."

The answer that they gave him
Left the mom and dad both cold,
"We're just making wooden bowls,
For when you and Mom get old."

Wooden Bowl

Abuse of parents has become a frequent occurrence in our fast-paced society. When parents become a burden, their children, or their children's spouses, often resent them. If the abuse and ridicule are carried on in front of the grandchildren, the parents may well find themselves treated in the same way when they become senior citizens. In the words of Barbara Bush, when asked about the antics of her grandchildren (The twin daughters of President Bush Jr.), "What goes around comes around."

THE MISSIONARY

He thought about the life he'd lived,
How he had spent it all for God.
How he had taught about God's love
And the many miles he had trod.

No time to have a family
And now his health was going fast.
He had passed the time allotted
But he'd labored until the last.

He had never made the papers
And worldly fame had passed him by.
His fare cost him all his savings,
Just to get home where he could die.

As he strolled along the ship's deck,
He happened to look in the bar.
There was a throng of people there,
Gathered around a movie star.

He had heard some people talking,
About her rapid rise to fame,
Just one movie made her famous
And now the whole world knew her name.

So he pondered the unjustness,
For he had given all he had.
He had gone where God had sent him,
Leaving his home while still a lad.

When at last they passed the Lady,
Standing there, with her torch held high,
He had held back his emotions
But now no longer would he try.

Then he saw a jubilant crowd,
One that stretched a whole city block.
A band played loud and banners waved,
As their ship pulled up to the dock.

A waving sign said, "Welcome home,
You have been away far too long."
While out in front a singing group
Burst forth into a happy song.

For an instant he had the thought
That God prepared this all for him.
But then the star appeared on deck
And his brief joy once more grew dim.

Then he began to question God
About rewards so clearly taught.
For the life he'd dedicated
And the all battles he had fought.

As he looked out over the crowd,
He could find no one to meet him.
He had written to his home church;
Wasn't someone there to greet him?

And then once more he questioned God
About how that he'd been treated.
One of God's servants coming home,
Is this how he should be greeted?

Then his answer came so clearly,
His expectations would be met.
God's loving voice in answer said,
"Don't you know that you're not home yet?"

The Missionary

Have you ever asked the question, "What has God ever done for me?" In a speech, President Kennedy once quoted, "Ask not what your country can do for you, rather ask what you can do for your country." This poem tells a story of how a tired servant of God was expecting some sort of welcome from his church, upon his arrival home from the mission field. God had to point out to him that praise from men was not something to be sought after and that his real home-coming had yet to occur. I'm sure that he was perfectly willing to wait a little longer for that particular celebration.

EXTRAVAGANZA

"It's time to go," the Father said,
As they all gathered at the gate.
They've been expecting us for years
And now we shouldn't make them wait.

The Son had all the maps and charts,
Taken from the Heavenly crypt.
Everything was going perfect
According to the ancient script.

The extravaganza was well planned,
The cast were all made ready.
Great expectation filled the air,
Heaven's atmosphere was heady.

The Program had been sent ahead
So very very long ago.
With every detail written down
For the chosen ones to go.

The event, so carefully planned,
Would start in very early morn.
When Gabriel, the supporting star,
Would stand and blow his golden horn.

Then Gabriel first expressed his doubt,
Would just his trumpet be enough?
With all the fancy shows on Earth,
The competition would be tough.

To counter all those big productions
Would take more than a Godly act.
"Can we compete with prime-time shows?"
Gabriel asked, with angel's tact.

"It might be best to hold our trip,
Maybe we should try for Monday,
A lot of folks will not show up
You know the Super Bowl is Sunday!"

Extravaganza

It is difficult for today's church to compete with the multimillion-dollar extravaganzas put on by the entertainment industry. Some churches try, with earthly offerings such as: people centers, tennis courts, bowling alleys and even swimming pools. The truly successful ones do so with the good old-fashion gospel message. Youth programs are necessary to attract youth but fund-raisers for a skiing trip should not dominate Bible study and worship time. In *Extravaganza*, I have posed the question; "How many Christians would be in favor of postponing the Rapture until after the Super Bowl game? While I'm on my soapbox, where did the phrase, "If God tarries, I'll do such and such," come from? My dictionary defines tarry as to linger or loiter. God is not loitering, He knows exactly when He's coming.

DEPARTURE

Last night I watched a ship depart,
As it sailed out to sea.
It took someone I loved away,
Who meant so much to me.

I thought of good times that we'd had
Together on this shore;
Experiences of a true friendship,
That we would share no more.

Sadness filled my aching heart,
Where joy had always been.
I knew that never in this life,
Would I see my friend again.

Then a comfort filled my soul
And I would grieve no more.
What joy my friend would bring to those
Who wait on that far shore.

Depature

I wrote *Departure* for a wonderful missionary friend, John Bell, when he went home to be with the Lord. Ruth and I spent our honeymoon at his home in beautiful Ikoma, Japan. He and his family have always been dear friends to us. As we get older, we see more and more of our friends leave us. I think that it was Mark Twain that said, he read the obituary column every morning and was always quite relieved to find that his name wasn't listed there. *Departure* is a nice poem to send to friends or relatives who have lost a loved one. It has been printed on the back of numerous funeral programs.

NO HELP NEEDED

The meeting was important.
He had driven twice around.
He needed a parking space,
There wasn't one to be found.

He began to pray out loud,
"Lord, find me a parking space
And I'll give up my drinking,
And spend Sundays at your place."

But God wasn't hearing him,
It was just as he had feared.
Too many others searching,
Then like magic one appeared

Now he would make his meeting
And he wouldn't have to run!
He said, "Just forget it God,
Because I just found me one!"

No Help Needed

How many times has God answered one of your prayers only to have the credit given to someone or something else? In *No Help Needed*, the guy surely wasn't going to give the credit to God, because then he would have to keep his promise. This type of promise is called a "Fox Hole Promise". I'm sure the reason why is apparent. You hear of promises, that were made in life or death situations, being kept and lives being changed as a result. Of course you never hear of the ones not kept.

CONUNDRUM

When Johnny was three our Christmas was fun.
We got up early to see what Santa had done.
That Santa existed he had little doubt,
For Santa had eaten the food we left out.

At four and at five he still was naive.
He was filled with excitement on each Christmas Eve.
But when he was six, he started to doubt.
We were sure he was going to find the truth out.

We had to be sneaky and tell little lies.
We just didn't want to spoil his surprise.
Not only for him, but also to please us,
Of course he was taught, the birthday of Jesus.

That was the true meaning we tried to impart,
If he was to have Jesus' love in his heart.
Then one day, after school, he sat down and cried.
His friends had told him that his parents had lied.

We tried to explain, the things we had done
Were to make him excited, to make Christmas fun.
We found out how hard our trust was to mend,
When we heard him discussing his hurt with a friend.

"No Santa Claus? No Easter Bunny?
They told me those lies and they think that it's funny?
I tell you just what, I'm gonna do.
I'm gonna check into this Jesus stuff too!"

Conundrum

OK, if you don't like *Conundrum*, tear the page out. Maybe I should have had the margin perforated to make it easy. While I was still in college, I heard this story from a Baptist minister who worked with the students. He claimed that it actually happened to him; since then he has been very careful about being truthful with his children, no matter how white the lie might seem to be. If we are untruthful with them, about someone as important in their lives as Santa Clause, it may cause them to think that we have been lying to them about God also. Every parent must make his or her own decision, on how to handle the Santa Clause conundrum.

NOT ENOUGH EVIDENCE

It was two in the morning when they kicked in our door.
A body's not safe in his home anymore.
They sure didn't knock or ring our doorbell.
Just what had we done? They weren't going to tell.

They put us in cuffs and took us down town,
Me in my 'jammas, my wife in her gown.
At last they explained; we were snatched out of bed
They had reason to believe, we were Christians, they said.

We sat in our cells not daring to pray,
For fear of just what other cellmates would say.
They checked all our records and questioned each friend;
We knew all was lost, that this was the end.

But then what they told us, as they said we could leave,
Didn't fill us with pride, it caused us to grieve.
Without further proof, they had no jurisdiction;
There wasn't enough evidence to get a conviction!

Not Enough Evidence

We've all heard the question, "If you were arrested for being a Christian, could they find enough evidence to convict you?" I thought that the saying would make an interesting poem and wrote *Not Enough Evidence* for this collection. It's not a bad idea to ask yourself that question about anything. For instance, if you were arrested for being a good parent, could they find enough evidence to convict you?

LINE UP

PERSPECTIVE

Two little goldfish,
Who lived in a bowl;
They thought that their home
Was the universe whole.

"Do you believe in God?"
One fish asked the other;
For neither was taught
By father or mother.

Then answered the son,
Or was it the daughter?
Of course there's a God;
He changes our water.

Perspective

Perspective, is about how two little goldfish perceive the world. Which is, as far as they are concerned, a little round bowl. Our perception of our world must look just as puny to God. I once heard a preacher say that if you put a goldfish, that has been confined to a small bowl all of its life, into a large pond, it will swim around in a small circle for several hours. As a fish farmer, I know that isn't so, but it was a good illustration of how we can let our perspective limit our abilities.

INDEX

BOOKS BY THE AUTHOR

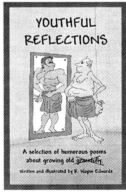

Printed in the United States
214959BV00004B/2/A